The United Nations in the 1990s

The United Nations in the 1990s

A Second Chance?

Max Jakobson

A TWENTIETH CENTURY FUND BOOK

Library of Congress Cataloging-in- Publication Data

Jakobson, Max.
    The United Nations in the 1990s, a second chance? / by Max Jakobson.

    p. cm.

    Includes index.
    ISBN 9211571855 $14.00
    1. United Nations. I. Title
JX1977.J25 1993
341.23—dc20   93-16216
                              CIP

FOREWORD

The end of the cold war may not have solved all the world's ills, but it certainly has changed the context in which nations seek to respond to them. With the likelihood of nuclear holocaust reduced, national leaders have a chance for a fresh start, for new hope, and even for experimentation. More specifically, the great transformation in global affairs provides a renewed opportunity for the idea of collective problem solving by the world nations.

At its inception, former Secretary of State Cordell Hull said that the United Nations was the instrument that would lead to "the fulfillment of humanity's highest aspirations and the very survival of our civilization." But the organization so widely hailed as a vehicle for improving the world spent many years caught up in a battle over conflicting ideologies. Now that has changed. So far, despite its mixed record and reputation, the United Nations has been the major institutional forum in which these new possibilities — and problems — of the post-cold war era are being tested.

The uncertain balance between new hopes and renewed threats is made more difficult to gauge, in part, by the simple fact that world politics looks so different. Indeed, the most striking events during the changes taking place in the former Soviet Union have been the eruption of old animosities, conflicts, and dangers, and the growing role of the international community in dealing with them. Moreover, the international response following the Iraqi invasion of Kuwait might have been very different before the Gorbachev revolution.

Statesmen and citizens are quite reasonably at a loss to know what to make of the changes that have taken place, as well as how to assess the future. Just as it has been painfully obvious in the case of Eastern Europe that we must look back and sort through the past in order to shape policies that might improve future prospects, it is

v

true that to understand the future of our international institutions, we must come to understand their history. When looking to the United Nations as the central forum and mechanism for dealing with global problems, we must take full account of the internal forces that continue to shape its responses and actions. In other words, our judgment about the institution's utility, at least for the immediate future, depends greatly upon our knowledge of the history and the balance of forces within this institution created by the World War II victors.

In Max Jakobson, former Finnish ambassador to the United Nations, we found the ideal individual to undertake the daunting task of both broadening our understanding of the problems that have in the past dimmed the light of this once promising institution and showing us how it can play a role in the post-cold war world. He brings a unique blend of long experience at the highest level of the United Nations and an understanding of statecraft to the task; for that, the Trustees and I thank him.

Richard C. Leone, *President*
THE TWENTIETH CENTURY FUND
February 1993

Table of Contents

INTRODUCTION

With the world in flux, an attempt to assess the future role of the United Nations in international affairs is like trying to fit a piece into a jigsaw puzzle that keeps shifting its shape. The forces of change that have shattered the postwar order have not subsided. No stability is in sight. Uncertainty about the future is as great as it was 120 years ago when the emergence of the first German Reich moved Benjamin Disraeli to make one of his most memorable pronouncements on world affairs:

> "Not a single principle in the management of our foreign affairs, accepted by all statesmen for guidance up to six months ago, any longer exists. There is not a diplomatic tradition which has not been swept away. You have a new world, new influences at work, new and unknown objects and dangers with which to cope . . ."[1]

Today, too, much of the conventional wisdom accumulated during almost half a century must be scrapped and many long-cherished political tenets reexamined.

The end of the cold war must mean the beginning of a new era. But so far no one has ventured to give the new a name. The international community of political analysts and commentators view the future with understandable caution. It has been severely chastened by its collective failure to foresee the changes that have shaken the world in the latter part of the 1980s. Each successive dying spasm of the old order has been met with cries of incredulous astonishment: Unthinkable! Unimaginable! None of us diplomats, journalists, scholars or spies was able to draw the right conclusion from the mass of information available to all. No government can claim to have anticipated the change, let alone to have directed or controlled it. Indeed, political leaders have been inclined not to believe what they actually could see happening.

1

Before making a new attempt to peer into the future, it might be useful to analyze the reasons for this lack of foresight. We were blinded by the facade of the totalitarian power structures: we believed they were invulnerable. We were overawed by the military capabilities of the superpowers and failed to assess them in a social and economic context. We counted missiles, but discounted the influence of people like Lech Walesa, Andrei Sakharov and Vaclav Havel. We underrated the vitality of nationalism — I use the term in a neutral sense — as a force stronger than ideological commitment. Having resigned ourselves to what were called the "political realities" of the postwar status quo, we did not grasp in time the explosive consequences of generational change which, combined with the communications revolution, have shattered the old order.

Most important, in my view, was our failure to foresee the social effect of the microelectronic revolution. On the Western side this is an old story: one more example of the gap between the Two Cultures. It is more surprising that the Soviet leaders were the last to grasp what was going on. Don't they read Karl Marx in Moscow? It was he, after all, who taught us to perceive the political implications of advances in the mode of production. What he wrote a hundred and fifty years ago about the consequences of the first industrial revolution has a topical ring today.

"The bourgeoisie," Marx wrote, "has accomplished wonders far surpassing Egyptian pyramids, Roman aqueducts, and Gothic cathedrals . . . The bourgeoisie has through its exploitation of the world market given a cosmopolitan character to production and consumption in every country. . . . All old-established national industries have been destroyed or are being destroyed. They are dislodged by new industries, whose introduction becomes a life-and-death question for all civilized nations. . . . In place of the old local and national seclusion and self-sufficiency, we have intercourse in every direction, universal interdependence of nations. . . . The bourgeoisie draws all, even the most backward, nations into civilization. It compels all nations on pain of extinction to adopt the bourgeois mode of production; it compels them to introduce what it calls civilization into their midst, that is, to become bourgeois themselves. In one word, it creates a world in its own image. . . ."[2]

With a change of a word here and there, this text could well serve as a description of what is going on in the world today. As in the 19th century, the old order is being undermined, not by any new political ideology or by an expansionist drive of an ambitious nation, but by the scientific and technological developments of the Information Age. As access to information and the ability to use it have become the crucial factors in economic progress, the open societies (market economies) have forged ahead; the closed societies (centrally planned economies) have been left behind. Technology has triumphed over ideology, the market has beaten Marx. According to one of the innumerable political jokes emanating from the Soviet Union, Karl Marx was given the chance to view the world as it is today and to address a global television audience. His message was: "Proletarians of the world, forgive me!"

Now, belatedly, Moscow is trying to catch up. A survey of Soviet foreign policy in the Gorbachev era from April 1985 to October 1989 prepared by the foreign ministry — in effect a declaration of unconditional surrender in the cold war — candidly admits that the Soviet Union was "very slow to respond to the strong and persistent signals of scientific and technological progress" which has "lent humanity a new quality." The survey goes on to state that "a dynamically developing economy based on new technology is becoming a key source of influence in the world." As a result, countries like the Soviet Union, which continue to depend on traditional industries and the production of raw materials, "are relegated to the role of involuntary tributaries of those whose might is based on investment in product of the human intellect." These changes are "hastening changes in the political sphere: the ideas of freedom and democracy, the supremacy of law and order, and freedom of choice are increasingly taking hold of peoples' thinking." As a result of the information revolution, "Individuals and peoples who are now in a position to compare things are demanding conditions and a quality of life that technological progress can provide."

As a consequence, the survey points out, the very concept of national security must be reexamined:

"No nation can consider itself secure unless it commands a powerful, dynamic economy. Those that have put the emphasis on military means are themselves at a disadvantage. . . . Military means of ensuring national security are objectively giving way to political and economic ones."[3]

The primacy of economic and social factors is graphically illustrated by what has taken place in Germany. It is called unification, but it would be more appropriate to call it a friendly take-over of a smaller, almost bankrupt firm by a bigger, more successful one. In 1938, Austria joined Germany under Hitler's threat to use his overwhelming military power to crush any resistance; today it is the attraction of the D-Mark and freedom that has persuaded the Germans in the East to join the West.

When socialist ideology lost its credibility, the East-German state simply collapsed; it had lost the reason of its existence. Similarly, the Soviet Union and Yugoslavia, both federations ostensibly held together by socialist ideology, are breaking up into their national components.

There is no doubt about who lost the cold war. But there is no sense of triumph on the winning side. Opinionmakers in the West are, as usual, tormented by self-doubt. The European Left has lost its illusion that the Soviet system could be reformed into socialism with a human face. The American Right has lost its enemy that for so long has provided a focus for its energies. Liberal democracy and the market economy or, more accurately, the mixed economy of the relatively small minority of the world population living in what are called developed countries is proving a frustratingly elusive model for the peoples now struggling to find their way out of the ruins of Soviet-style socialism. It is not like a ready made suit one can pick off the peg. With Western assistance the former socialist countries of Europe may make it, but many Third World nations whose leaders now switch their allegiance to the winning side are bound to suffer set-backs and disappointment. The end of the cold war will not make the world safe for democracy; more likely the void left by the failure of socialist dreams will be filled in large parts of the world by nationalist, fundamentalist and authoritarian currents.

In the developed world, too, governments will be grappling with global market forces that none of them is able wholly to control, while facing the increasingly pressing need to take concerted action to deal with ecological and environmental concerns.

It is against this background that the future prospects of the United Nations must be examined: Is it an institutional dinosaur doomed to slow extinction or will it be able to survive by adapting itself to changing world conditions?

It may seem that this question has already been conclusively answered by the resolute response of the UN Security Council in August 1990 to the aggression committed by Iraq against Kuwait. At last the Council has shown itself capable of forceful collective action, as prescribed by the Charter. At the Helsinki Summit in September 1990, Presidents George Bush and Mikhail Gorbachev presented a common front in defense of international legality. Does this not mean that President Roosevelt's vision of a world order maintained by the "Five Policemen" — the permanent members of the Security Council — has finally become reality?

UN Secretary-General Javier Pérez de Cuellar has gone so far as to claim, in his report to the General Assembly in September 1990, that "nothing in the great changes that have taken place in world conditions requires a modification of the purposes and principles of the Organization as laid down in the Charter" and that the UN "enters the post-cold war era as a central point of constancy" in the midst of change.

The conflict in the Persian Gulf has indeed shown that once the five permanent members reach agreement the UN can be used effectively as an instrument of collective action to keep or restore order in international relations. But this had been proved already during the previous period of US-Soviet détente in the late 1960s and early 1970s, when the Great Satan of Imperialism and the Evil Empire found it convenient to seek from the UN a cover of legitimacy for their collaboration in pacifying the Third World, and then again more systematically from 1987 onward, when the Security Council began to deal with the regional conflicts that had been fuelled by the cold war. It would be an illusion, however, to believe that the UN could now take a "great leap backward" to 1945 by reviving the collective security system designed in San Francisco and kept deep-frozen during the decades of the cold war. The action taken against Iraq, far from demonstrating the continued viability of that system, has on the contrary revealed the total collapse of the power structure on which the 1945 design was based.

Roosevelt's Five Policemen are no longer in charge. The Soviet Union is in a state of decomposition and likely to be absorbed in a variety of conflicts within its own borders. It will hardly be a credible partner in efforts to solve the troubles of other countries. China cannot be expected, in the foreseeable future, to exercise much influence beyond its immediate vicinity. Britain and France, two medium-weight powers, will remain preoccupied with European issues for many years to come. Thus, of the five, one lone ranger remains: the United States as the only superpower with a global military reach. But economically the United States is a superpower living on credit. In the Gulf crisis it has had to solicit funds from the two new economic superpowers, Japan and Germany, neither of which shares the responsibility for the maintenance of international peace and security that the UN Charter assigns to the five permanent members of the Security Council.

In the case of Iraq versus Kuwait — an exceptionally flagrant instance of armed robbery — the national interest of the United States in safeguarding its oil supplies happily coincides with the collective interest in upholding the rule of law. But next time the two interests may diverge, and we may then see either unilateral American action without UN endorsement or UN resolutions without enough power behind them.

There is another reason why it is premature to hail the Security Council decision on Iraq's aggression against Kuwait as a great victory for collective security. It is in fact an attempt to reverse a self-inflicted failure. The five permanent members themselves bear a heavy responsibility for the conflict in the Persian Gulf. Not only did they fail to punish Saddam Hussein for his aggression against Iran, they rewarded him for it by supplying him with the best weapons money can buy, thus giving him every reason to assume that by attacking Kuwait he would risk nothing worse than a limp slap on the wrist. Having themselves built him up into a Frankenstein's monster, the Five Policemen were left with no choice but resort to economic sanctions backed up with a threat of military intervention — a blunt and heavy instrument the use of which in today's interdependent world tends to create a host of new problems and conflicts in its wake.

A collective security system worth its name should deter and prevent aggression. The cold war order, flawed and fragile as it was, did that, up to a point. It depended on the authority and ability of the two superpowers to maintain a sufficient degree of discipline within their respective spheres of influence in order to prevent or contain conflicts that might undermine the central balance of power between the two blocs. The fact that on the Soviet side discipline was maintained by brutal repression of national independence and human rights did not stop the Western world from enjoying the benefits of a stable international order. The collapse of Soviet power has brought immense gains in terms of freedom for nations and of human rights. But it has also left a power vacuum which cannot be filled by the United States alone. There is thus an obvious need to make the UN collective security system work. But the 1945 system is no longer adequate. It must be redesigned to reflect the realities of power prevailing in the 1990s and beyond.

In light of the profound changes that have taken place in international relations since 1945, some of the basic assumptions underlying the UN system must be reexamined. The Charter reflects a view of the world in which states are static, self-contained units, separate from each other like so many billiard balls, interacting primarily through their governments, each of which is supposed to be in sovereign control over its own territory and people. The principle of non-interference in the internal affairs of states is the cornerstone of the Charter: "Nothing contained in the present Charter shall authorize the United Nations to intervene in matters which are essentially within the domestic jurisdiction of any state . . ." (Article 2:7). Security, according to the Charter, is a military concept. Threats to peace or breaches of the peace are caused solely by military aggression in the classical sense — the armies of one state marching across an international border into another state. The collective security system of the Charter is in fact designed to stop a new Hitler or Mussolini — most recently in the form of Saddam Hussein. While generals are always planning to win the last war, diplomats are trying to prevent it.

The world of the Charter of course never actually existed. It is a legal fiction governments find convenient to pretend to believe in. Today, pretense is no longer possible. The relentless advance of economic integration and the power of modern communications have rendered Article 2:7 meaningless. The billiard balls have gone soft and porous. With the one exception of Iraq v. Kuwait, all the conflicts currently on the agenda of the Security Council are complex issues arising from internal causes within states and riddled with moral ambiguity — the Middle-East, Cambodia, Cyprus, Central-America, Afghanistan. None quite fits the models envisaged in the Charter; none could be settled by bludgeoning the parties into submission by the military might of the five permanent members. In fact, in recent years the Security Council has begun to employ more subtle methods of conflict resolution.

The concept of international peace and security can no longer be defined exclusively in military terms. The growing gap between the diminishing minority of wealthy nations — today about 20% of the global population — and the poor, now including the Soviet Union and the former socialist states of Europe, is the main source of instability, disorder and various degrees of violence. The void at the center created by the collapse of Soviet power and the contraction of United States overseas commitments, if not filled by a collective authority, is likely to lead to a further proliferation of nuclear and chemical weapons and long-range missiles, to the collapse of regimes swelling the stream of refugees and migrations, to more ethnic conflict, more terrorism, more drugs — in a word, a world out of control. Such a world will be incapable of organizing the kind of coordinated and sustained action that has become urgently necessary to safeguard the future functioning of the natural systems on which life on this crowded planet ultimately depends.

With great agility world public opinion — by which is meant the current collective anguish of the opinionmakers of the most advanced countries — has switched its eschatological concern from nuclear war to ecological catastrophe, from a nuclear winter to the greenhouse effect: either way, it seems, the End is near. The new password to the circle of the well-informed is chlorofluorocarbon.

The call for drastic action to save civilization grows more insistent. According to Sir Brian Urquhart, a man who has spent forty years at the center of the UN, "If we are to take survival for granted, governments will have to make a determined and conscious leap forward in their international behaviour."[4] But if we are to believe the late Konrad Lorenz, the great ethnologist, we will have to wait a very long time for such a leap: "We are governed by men with a genetic make-up which has not changed since the later stone age."[5]

If we men of the late stone age are by nature too primitive to rise above our aggressive instincts and selfish greed, must we not be forced by a supranational authority to submit to a new world order that will ensure survival? As has been pointed out by one of its advocates, the German physicist Karl Friedrich von Weizsacker, such a world order would have to be a harsh dictatorship: If freedom and survival clash, it is freedom that must yield.[6] But how a world authority could be established and who might run it are questions the visionaries leave unanswered.

For as far into the future as we can see, the world will remain organized as it is today: sovereign states will continue to be the basic units of the international system. Nevertheless the growing interdependence between states is bound to intensify the debate on how to reconcile sovereignty and national self-determination with the need to organize collective action for common ends. This issue implicitly heads every UN agenda.

Sovereignty is an elusive concept — a kaleidoscope with constantly shifting reflections. In the fall of 1988, for instance, presidential candidate George Bush felt the need to assure his supporters that as president he would "not sacrifice one ounce of United States sovereignty to the UN." Now, two years later, with the Persian Gulf crisis at hand, Americans are looking to the UN as an effective defense against aggression. But it is not only Americans who use a double standard in judging the UN. Almost everybody expects the UN to make other nations behave, while insisting on keeping the sovereignty of his own state intact.

On a philosophical level, sovereignty comes under attack from both ends of the ideological spectrum. On the one hand it is claimed that technology has rendered sovereignty obsolete. As currency rates, for instance, are being determined by some thousands of dealers operating a global electronic exchange, the real sovereign is the market. On the other hand it is claimed that national governments have too much sovereignty for their own good and ought to submit to supranational authority in order to curb and control global market forces.

It is misleading, however, to equate sovereignty with the extent of government control over the national economy or the activities of citizens. An historical example will illustrate the fallacy of this argument. In the beginning of this century the government of Great Britain exercised minimal control over business and industry or the lives of individuals. A law-abiding British subject could live all his life without contact with any government institution, except the post office. Not only British subjects but also foreigners could enter and leave the country without passport and reside there without having to register with the police. Was Great Britain at that time less sovereign than it was after the second world war when government control was extended across the entire economy and society?

As for nation-states submitting to supranational authority, in the European Community for instance, this only transfers sovereignty to a federal authority, which would not necessarily turn out to be a more constructive, less "nationalistic" partner in global collective actions for the common good.

National governments are indeed losing control — within their own borders. This is happening dramatically in the Soviet Union and elsewhere where totalitarian regimes are losing their hold over subject nations. But in Western Europe, too, the stubborn facts of national and regional differences are emerging through the smokescreen of federalist rhetoric. With the rise of educational levels and the pervasive influence of communications, people everywhere are insisting on more direct political influence. It is now recognized within the European Community that a delegation of power to a supranational authority must be accompanied by an extension of common democratic institutions: The Brussels bureaucrats must be made accountable to a European parliament. But how long will it take before the twelve different nations of the European Community speaking fifteen different languages with at least three main cultural streams and different legal systems can achieve the necessary degree of political unity for the creation of a common parliamentary institution?

In the United Nations, state sovereignty until now has been sacrosanct. It is the last refuge of the great majority of member states — the weak and the poor. The powerful and rich states — the "developed countries" — can afford to "pool" their sovereignty, for they know they themselves will determine how the pool will work. The weak and the poor states — the "developing countries" — know they will have little say in any supranational context. They cling to sovereignty, however illusory it may be in reality, as a shield against domination.

So far the developed countries have, on the whole, allowed the developing countries to keep their illusion, which is why so much of what is going on in the UN has an air of unreality. Now this is changing. The developed countries are no longer constrained by the cold war, giving them greater leverage in dealing with the developing countries. In return for economic aid these countries will have to submit to stricter arms control, become more democratic and show greater respect for human rights. They will also have to conform to what is called acceptable environmental conduct. Radical changes in economic and social policies are clearly in the offing. As the East-West confrontation fades away, center stage at the UN will be taken over by a number of interrelated issues of great complexity — population, economic development, energy, and environment. They are bound to be the source of much tension and turbulence in the 1990s.

As a consequence, public interest which now is focused on issues relating to international security is likely to broaden to take in the entire range of UN activities. Obviously, the UN cannot live by peacekeeping alone — an activity that absorbs a relatively small proportion of its total organizational resources. The large majority of all the people employed by the UN are busy with other tasks.

The image conjured up by the letters UN in the minds of most people is one of a glittering glass tower with thirty-eight floors and a conference hall where delegates of different races in varying postures of boredom listen to speeches through earphones. In fact, of course, the UN is shorthand for a sprawling complex of great variety of organizations comprising what is commonly called the UN system or the UN family, although in actual fact it lacks both the orderly character of a system and the cozy intimacy of a family. I prefer family, because all its component parts are related (some rather too closely) and they quarrel as fiercely as only family members do.

The UN proper, the parent organization as it were, disposes over more than four billion dollars annually, one third of which is used for humanitarian purposes, mainly on behalf of refugees, and another third for operational activities in the field of economic and social development. It has established over the past decade a large number of subsidiary bodies. Everyone knows UNICEF, the children's fund; less known are the Industrial Development Organization (UNIDO), the Conference on Trade and Development (UNCTAD), the Development Program (UNDP), the High Commissioner for Refugees (UNHCR), the Relief and Works Agencies for Palestinian Refugees (UNRWA), and the World Food Program (WFP); only a few specialists could list the additional thirty-odd juridically independent funds, institutes, centers and councils.

Then there are the specialized agencies with their own separate constitutions, memberships and budgets. Some of them, like the Educational, Scientific and Cultural Organization (UNESCO), the Food and Agriculture Organization (FAO), the International Labor Organization (ILO), and the World Health Organization (WHO), tend to roam well beyond their particular sector across the entire field of economic and social problems and even political and ideological issues, while the organizations charged with operating regulatory systems in such fields as postal services, telecommunications and transportation, stick to their technical functions. The

International Atomic Energy Agency (IAEA) is another separate and important intergovernmental organization associated with the UN.

In a formal sense, the financial organizations — the International Monetary Fund (IMF), the International Bank for Reconstruction and Development (IBRD) and its affiliates, as well as the General Agreement of Tariffs and Trade (GATT) — are also counted as members of the UN family. In practice, however, the connection is tenuous. These organizations differ in two important respects from other UN organizations: The Soviet Union is not a member, and the voting system is weighted in a manner that ensures the dominant position of the United States. But now that the Soviet Union and other former socialist countries are prepared to join, the role of these agencies will change.

To try to follow what the various members of the UN family actually do and to determine how well each performs its tasks is an Herculean undertaking. The media is of no help. They mainly ignore what is going on in the UN, except on the rare occasion when the major powers choose to use the Security Council as the forum for important decisions or some incident provides a brief flash of drama.

This does not by itself prove that the UN is unimportant. Editorial judgement on what is fit to print is often erratic, superficial or even frivolous. Diplomacy, when successfully practiced, is devoid of news value. The media looks for stories with drama and action; the UN proceedings are the diplomatic equivalent of a stream of consciousness, with no beginning and no end. The media likes colorful, quotable speeches; UN debates offer the infinite boredom of carefully drafted official statements. The media asks for results, but the influence exercised by the UN can seldom be measured by the results, or lack of them, in any given situation. Rather, it must be judged by the process itself — the never-ending flow of consultations designed to advance mutual understanding and reconcile different interests. Like the Glass Bead of Herman Hesse's novel, the UN has developed "a kind of universal language through which the players can express values and set these in relation to one another." But outsiders have difficulty in decoding the messages exchanged by UN insiders.

The lack of media interest in the UN has political consequences. What editors and commentators consider too unimportant
to warrant attention inevitably slides downward on the scales of
political priorities. The attitude of the media thus not only mirrors,
but also reinforces the view widely held among UN diplomats and
international civil servants that much of what they do has little
impact on the reality of international relations and only marginally
affects the decisions and actions of member states.

Paradoxically, the marginalization of the UN has taken place
at a time when the growing interdependence of nations creates an
ever greater need for closer cooperation. This need spawns new
organizations at an increasing rate, but outside of the UN. By one
count, the number of intergovernmental organizations of global or
regional scope is now 340 and increases every year by about ten,
while the number of non-governmental organizations dealing with
international issues has reached 4500 and is increasing by about 200
annually.[7] This development responds to the profound changes in
international relations in the past decades and need not in itself
detract from the importance of the UN as the universal political
framework for international cooperation. But seen against the
background of a diminishing interest in the UN, it does carry a
warning message: The customers are turning elsewhere for better
service.

A business enterprise in a similar situation would have to
improve its products or go out of business. The UN does not run
such a risk. The UN system has become part of the international
structure. Like the welfare state, it will continue to be criticized on
the grounds that it is inefficient or in parts redundant, and some of
its activities may be cut down, as happened with UNESCO, but
barring a global upheaval, it will not be dismantled. The worst that
can happen to the UN is that it will be left as it is. But that is bad
enough: it would mean continued stagnation.

In an insider's view, "There is really nothing wrong with the
UN — except its members."[8] The phrase repeated time and again
in discussions on the decline of the UN is "lack of political will." By
this is meant that governments more often than not fail to carry out
the highminded resolutions they vote for. The pursuit of narrowly

conceived national interest stands in the way of more enlightened action for the common good.

The banal truth that the UN can do no more than its members wish it to do cannot be repeated too often. Yet like all institutions of its kind, the UN has acquired a life of its own. It has not kept up with the rapid change in world conditions. Part of its machinery is hopelessly out of touch with present-day realities. This is especially true in the economic and social sector.

Indeed, listening to what the experts have to say about the state of the UN, as I have done in the course of working on this book, is a fairly melancholy experience. It brings to mind the sad fate of those fine old townhouses originally designed for gracious living, which have been divided and redivided into pokey little apartments and occupied by large families with badly behaved children and strange cooking habits. The more prosperous tenants have moved elsewhere, and the owners refuse to pay for necessary repairs, leaving the poor janitor to take the blame for the failures of an antiquated plumbing system. The rational thing to do would be to tear the house and build a new structure better suited for present-day conditions. But for sentimental reasons, or simply lack of energy, nothing is done and the place is left to decay.

One reason the UN has been allowed to decline has been the lack of United States interest. A revealing insight into what the UN looks like from the point of view of Washington decision-makers is provided by detailed accounts of the conduct of United States foreign policy during the twelve years of the Nixon and Carter presidencies in Henry Kissinger's and Zbigniew Brzezinski's respective memoirs.[9] Each volume contains scattered references to the UN — Kissinger mentions it fewer than 100 times in 2700 pages, Brzezinski fewer than fifty in 585 pages. Neither author has anything to say about the UN as an instrument of policy or generally as an institution with any substantive influence on international affairs. The evidence, circumstantial as it is, supports the conclusion that, in the twelve years covered, those at the center of power in Washington looked upon the UN as a secondary venue, used occasionally (as during the Pakistan-India war in 1971 or the Arab-Israel war in 1973) as a complement to the main action, but at no time as a matter of high priority. In retrospect, the Nixon-Carter period can be seen as one of benign neglect of the UN, to be followed by scornful rejection under President Ronald Reagan.

This is now changing. After an initial period of indifference, the Bush administration clearly upgraded the UN on its scale of priorities. In September 1989 the State Department praised the UN for "making a constructive and practical contribution to world peace — more so than at any other time in its forty-four year history." It called for a new effort to enhance the Organization's effectiveness by what it called a "unitary" approach designed to rationalize the UN system. A year later, on October 3, 1990, a joint US-Soviet statement was issued reaffirming the determination of the two governments to work for a more effective UN. One step to this end, according to the statement, would be for member states to pay their dues to the Organization on time. The United States for its part has made a pledge to pay off its arrears of 500 million dollars in five annual installments. No doubt the UN response to the Iraqi aggression against Kuwait will help turn Congressional opinion in favor of appropriating the necessary funds. UN.

Active American involvement — in terms of political interest, personnel and money — is prerequisite to successful reform of the UN. The United States today is still the member state with the greatest world wide influence and interests. It is by far the largest single contributor to the total UN-system budget (1.25 billion dollars in 1989). No other state or combination of states could provide the necessary leadership. The future of the UN will thus hinge on whether the reawakened American interest can be sustained over the coming years.

Even with strong American input, reform will be difficult. To call for a "unitary approach" is a revolutionary idea. Any serious attempt to rationalize the UN system will run into stubborn resistance from a variety of vested interests. But leadership must also come from within the Organization itself. This is why the choice of the next Secretary-General will be of crucial importance.

There is today a real opportunity to reshape the world organization into a more effective instrument for common action.

This second chance has been created by the extraordinary confluence of the fundamental interests of all the major power centers in the world. The United States has rediscovered the usefulness of the UN as a ready-made mechanism of burden-sharing on a global scale. For the Soviet Union, a country desperately in need of a stable international environment, the UN offers a chance to hold on to some degree of influence over international developments. Japan, as the world's leading trading power, has an obvious interest in playing a more active role in efforts to create a more reliable world order. Western Europe can be counted to continue to act in the same direction. China, absorbed as she is in her own affairs, is no longer a revolutionary influence. The countries of the Third World, with very few exceptions, have turned inward to deal with their own overwhelming problems.

A renewal of the UN may be helped along by the generational cycle. Men and women for whom the second world war is distant history are holding positions of leadership. They are unencumbered by the dreams of their grandparents or the disillusionment of their parents. To them, the UN is not a god that failed — an unsuccessful attempt to replace the brutal and sordid game of power politics with the rule of law and respect for moral principle. They are able to see the UN more objectively as part of the complex system of shifting relationships between states — partnerships, dependencies, rivalries, disputes and conflicts; as one means among several available to governments for the joint management of their common interests. A realistic conception could finally liberate the UN from the curse of inflated expectations that has plagued it from its inception.

The new generation is not likely to respond to a call for a strengthening of the UN for its own sake, as the only right road to salvation. It is more likely to listen to the cool voice of practical advantage: Ask not what we can do for the UN, ask what the UN can do for us. What services can the organization render in the 1990s and what must be done to improve its effectiveness in performing the tasks assigned to it?

I

FROM KOREA TO KUWAIT

Among the many sentimental anecdotes recalling the lost world of imperial Russia there is the one about the lonely sentry posted regularly, year after year, to stand guard over a remote spot in the park surrounding the Czar's summer palace at Tsarskoye Selo outside St. Petersburg, where Empress Alexandra once during a walk had come across an early spring flower and ordered an aide to make sure no one would step on it. The flower had died, but no one had remembered to withdraw the sentry.

In the UN, too, flowers that long ago have lost their bloom are faithfully guarded. Its aversion to institutional change is probably second only to that of the House of Lords of the British Parliament. Hardly any item is ever removed from the agenda and very few committees are disbanded after completing their assignment.

The prime example of the extreme conservatism of the UN is the curious case of the five colonels — an American, a British, a Chinese, a French and a Soviet — who for more than forty years have met every two weeks at the UN for the sole purpose of recording the fact that they have nothing to discuss. They constitute the Military Staff Committee (MSC), a body until recently forgotten by all but a few experts, which according to Article 47 of the Charter "shall consist of the chiefs of staff of the permanent members of the Security Council or their representatives." Their task is to "advise and assist the Security Council on all questions relating to the Security Council's military requirements for the maintenance of international peace and security, the employment and command of forces placed at its disposal, the regulation of armaments, and possible disarmament."

For a brief time after the end of the second world war the MSC actually functioned as envisaged in the Charter, but the cold war put an end to that, and from 1946 until August 1990 its meetings have lasted only a few minutes at a time: an organ kept alive by artificial respiration.

The case of the five colonels cannot be dismissed simply as one of the many absurdities produced by bureaucratic inertia. The unwillingness of any of the five powers to pull the plug and so take upon itself the onus of dismantling the security system of the UN Charter reveals the existence somewhere deep down, underneath layers of mutual suspicion and hostility, of a rockbed of common interest between the victors of the second world war. In Moscow, at any rate, nostalgia for the wartime alliance with the United States has survived all the crises and tensions of the past four decades. And now Soviet leader Mikhail Gorbachev's proposals for a revitalization of the UN include the idea of activating the Military Staff Committee.

This takes us back to an after-dinner conversation at the White House in May 1942. The guest President Franklin D. Roosevelt entertained that night was Vyacheslav Molotov, the foreign minister of the Soviet Union. This was Molotov's first visit to Washington, and he had taken the precaution of bringing a pistol along. Legend has it that he tucked it under his pillow before going to bed in an upstairs family bedroom in the White House. Often interpreted as evidence of his extreme suspicion towards his hosts, it may have been simply the habit of a lifetime, like saying one's evening prayer at bedtime.

As it turned out, carrying a pistol was quite appropriate for the role his host had in mind for the Soviet Union in the postwar world. What Roosevelt told Molotov after their first dinner was that he thought "the United States, Russia, England and possibly China should police the world and enforce disarmament by inspection after the war." The President pointed out that the population of the Four Policemen was well over a billion people, so together they could maintain law and order throughout the world. "Since small nations were incapable of defending themselves against powerful aggressors, they might just as well remain unarmed after the war, thus relieving their people of a heavy economic burden. If any of them were to try to violate the prohibition against armaments, the policing powers could then threaten to quarantine the offending state and, if that did not work, to bomb some part of it." When Molotov asked if this was the President's "final and considered judgement," Roosevelt answered affirmatively and asked Molotov to communicate his ideas to Stalin. Two days later, at another White House conference, Molotov informed the President that Stalin approved Roosevelt's proposal that the Big Four police the world. "This idea," Molotov said, "had the full approval of the Soviet government, which would support it fully."[1]

This was how the UN was born. Roosevelt's concept of the collective security system was elaborated upon; the idea of disarming the smaller states was abandoned. "The eagles must let the smaller birds sing," Winston Churchill said at the Yalta conference in 1945, adding however that the eagles need not take much notice of what the smaller birds might be singing. So the smaller states were given a voice and a vote each in the General Assembly which has the right to make recommendations. But Roosevelt's Four Policemen, later joined by France as a fifth, were placed firmly in charge of international peace and security. The Security Council was empowered, in Article 42 of the Charter, to make decisions binding upon all member states, to order economic sanctions, or blockades, or "take such action by air, sea or landforces as may be necessary to maintain or restore international peace and security." Thus the organs of the wartime alliance were transplanted into the body of the organization for peace.

As we now know, the idea of the five powers acting collectively was perverted by the cold war into a division of the world into spheres of influence, with each of the five attempting to maintain law and order in its own precinct. And each has been humiliated: Britain in Suez, France in Indochina and Algeria, the United States in Vietnam, the Soviet Union in Afghanistan. Yet, at the end of the second world war, Roosevelt's concept was generally accepted as the only realistic way to ensure peace. A world ruled by Five Policemen seemed preferable to a world ruled by one madman. At the time no one could doubt the capacity of the Five Policemen to enforce their decisions. The war effort had concentrated control over national resources into the hands of the governments. At the end of the war the armed forces of the Grand Alliance were the masters of the world. At Yalta the Big Three were able to redraw the map of Europe and Asia. Their arrogance was backed by overwhelming power.

The fifty-two delegations that gathered in San Francisco in 1945 to endorse the collective security system worked out among the big powers under American leadership represented a relatively homogeneous community of established states. The great majority were European or North and South American bound together by a common view of history. This view was shaped by the European experience, where the rivalries between the powers had caused two world wars. A third world war had to be prevented by an effective security system that would stop the kind of aggression practiced by Hitler and Mussolini.

Yet, from the outset, Europe was declared out of bounds for the UN. A short chapter of the Charter entitled "Transitional Security Arrangements" (Articles 106 and 107) acknowledges the exclusive right of Britain, France, the Soviet Union and the United States to deal with the postwar settlement in Europe. These transitional arrangements stayed in force for forty-five years. The American and Soviet armies remained in winter quarters in the heart of Europe, facing each other across the line where the allied armies had met in May 1945.

According to conventional wisdom, peace in Europe has been maintained by the deterrent effect of nuclear weapons. But the relationship between the two alliances has not been solely confrontational or adversarial. They have also been bound together by bonds of complicity. Each had built up its military, political and economic institutions on the basis of the division of Germany — the rockbed of common interest. What in 1945 was thought to be transitional became an integral part of the European structure. Neither side wished to upset it. It is revealing that the German question or the status of Berlin — central issues of the cold war — were never placed on the agenda of the UN. European affairs have never been considered in a substantive way in the UN. (Soviet interventions in Hungary and Czechoslovakia were debated, but no serious effort was made to settle these conflicts within a UN framework.)

While Europe remained frozen in the mold shaped by the military outcome of the second world war, everywhere else the world of 1945 was swept away by revolutionary change. It did not take long before the Five Policemen began to accuse each other of the kind of crimes against the international order that they were supposed jointly to prevent. One of the Five, the Chiang Kai-shek regime in China, lost power in its own country. The British and French empires disintegrated. The cold war between the United States and the Soviet Union paralysed the UN as an instrument of cooperation among the big powers and transformed it into a battleground between two opposing ideologies and power blocs.

Yet, even at moments of supreme tension between the superpowers, indeed precisely at such moments, the UN could be used to defuse a critical situation. The Hungarian crisis in October 1956 is a case in point. As Soviet tanks rolled into Budapest to crush the Hungarian uprising, the United States put before the Security Council a resolution demanding that the Soviet Union desist from further military action and withdraw from Hungary. As expected, a Soviet veto prevented the Council from taking a decision, after which the General Assembly by a large majority condemned the Soviet action and then went on to request the Secretary-General "to investigate the situation and to bring an end to the foreign intervention in Hungary" — another mission impossible. So it was the UN, not the United States, that had let the Hungarians down — a fig leaf to cover America's embarrassment.

The Cuban missile crisis in 1962 provides another illustration. Soviet leader Nikita Khrushchev, faced with the American demand for the removal from Cuba of the Soviet missiles, chose to yield by way of accepting the appeal made by Secretary-General U Thant rather than submitting directly to President Kennedy's ultimatum. As an American UN diplomat has pointed out, "The UN made a significant ancillary contribution to achieving a peaceful solution. It provided a forum for rallying the moral support of other governments and a convenient site for behind-the-scenes negotiations between American and Soviet representatives."[2] U Thant's offer of UN services for verifying the removal of the missiles was also accepted by the United States and the Soviet Union, but it was then rejected by Castro and the United States had to use its own means of verification.

There are other less dramatic examples of the use made by governments of the UN as a safety valve, to establish an alibi for not taking the violent action an incensed domestic opinion is clamoring for, to climb down from a limb to back out of a fight without loss of face. As representative of Finland on the Security Council, I was personally involved in one such case, when in August 1970 the government of the Republic of Ireland requested that a UN peacekeeping force be sent to pacify Northern Ireland where a serious outbreak of violence had just occurred. Public opinion in the Republic of Ireland was incensed, and the government could not stand by and do nothing. So the Foreign Minister, Patrick Hillery, was sent to New York to put the Irish case to the Security Council. He knew, and we all knew, that the British would veto any proposal for a UN intervention in what they considered a matter within the domestic jurisdiction of the United Kingdom. But I could not help thinking that it would be wrong to send the Irish foreign minister home without even giving him a chance to state his case. Surely such a humiliating end to his mission would further inflame emotions in Ireland and possibly force the government to measures that would make matters worse. So I proposed that the Council, contrary to established practice, should let the Irish foreign minister state his case before deciding whether or not it was competent to deal with the matter. This was approved, Mr. Hillery made his speech, and his government could claim that it had put the case of the Irish people before the highest organ of the world community. This episode, according to a British historian of the Security Council, "admirably illustrates a way in which an apparently empty exchange of words in the Council, leading to no formal agreement or action, can sometimes help to stabilize a dangerous situation."[3]

This ritual function, which has been called the "sacred drama" of reconciliation, might seem like a cynical charade. Yet it fills an obvious need. Every community, from the most primitive to the most advanced, has its symbolic ceremonies which enable opposing parties to act out, instead of fighting out, their conflicts. In one African tribe a priest with a leopard's skin swung around the right shoulder — an impressive badge of office in a society where the men wear no clothing at all — might intervene between opposing groups by cutting a line with a hoe and forbidding either side to cross it.[4] A Security Council resolution may serve a similar purpose. The ritual is useful for "directing aggression into harmless channels and thus inhibiting actions that are injurious to the survival of the species." I quote this from Konrad Lorenz's definition of the purpose of symbolic ceremonies performed by birds. The human species has not yet developed the choreography of its face-saving ceremonies to the level of perfection achieved by cranes, but some of the procedures evolved in the UN represent the first halting steps in that direction.

The point should not be stretched too far, however. It cannot be assumed that, had there been no UN, President Eisenhower would have unleashed a nuclear war over Hungary or that Khrushchev would not have found some other way to accede to the American demands on Cuba. Since the UN was never meant to be an arbiter in disputes between the major powers, its role in the context of the Soviet-American confrontation could be no more than marginal.

Instead, the real significance of the UN during the first quarter century of its history lies in the part it played in the dismantling of colonial empires, a process that has transformed international relations to an extent no one had foreseen in 1945. Of course, colonial rule would have come to an end in any event, with or without the UN, but without it the process might well have been less orderly. The UN provided decolonization with an organizational and ideological framework, and it offered the new states instant international recognition and a ready-made platform for making their needs and aspirations known to the world. They used it to turn the attention of the Organization in new directions, away from the issues of the cold war. They insisted on giving priority to the need to free the peoples still living under colonial rule, fight racial oppression and, above all, help the poor nations to develop economically. To those directly affected, progress in these directions seems painfully slow. In historical perspective, however, the campaign waged through the UN to persuade rich nations to accept the goals of economic development, racial equality, and decolonization had an unprecedented success.

The turmoil caused by the emergence of more than a hundred new member states from Africa, Asia and the Caribbean region presented the UN with a wide variety of conflicts which failed to conform to the models designed in San Francisco. With few exceptions, they have not been the kind of classical wars between states that have been fought in Europe — that is, armies marching across international borders from one country into another. They have been conflicts arising from the withdrawal of imperial power, the division of nations along ideological lines, disputes over legitimacy, violent internal conflicts — or a combination of such causes — conflicts like Korea, Indochina, Palestine, Cyprus, Kashmir, Angola.

In the face of the violent upheavals in the Third World the enforcement powers granted by the UN Charter to the Five Policemen for the removal of a threat to peace or suppression of aggression remained unused. (The use of mandatory economic sanctions in the late 1960s to force the white regime in Southern Rhodesia — now Zimbabwe — to share power with the black majority is not applicable in this connection. This was not a case of aggression in the accepted sense of the term; it was a human rights issue.)

In the Third World there has been no rockbed of common interest between the United States and the Soviet Union. It has been virgin land open to competitive drives for ideological, strategic or economic gain. Each side has tried to use the UN for its own advantage in the struggle for the mastery of the Third World.

The Birth of Peacekeeping

During the first two decades of its existence the UN was described, with a great deal of justification, as an auxiliary of the US State Department. The problem for American policymakers was how to get around the Soviet veto in the Security Council. The solution was to build up the General Assembly as an alternative. The first moves in this direction were made as early as November 1947. As an American UN expert has put it, "The Assembly became an important forum for denouncing Soviet actions, mobilizing the pressures of world opinion, clarifying US positions, and enlisting the support of the international community for policies the United States was undertaking or contemplating."[5]

As it happened, the General Assembly was not needed when the UN faced its first big test — the North Korean invasion of South Korea in June 1950. Since the Soviet Union at the time was boycotting the Security Council to protest the continued presence of Chiang Kai-shek's representative in the seat of China, the decision authorizing the United States to take military action in the name of the UN in defense of South Korea could be adopted without a veto. But in August 1950 the Soviet representative returned to the Security Council, and two months later the United States introduced what became known as the "Uniting for Peace" resolution, giving the General Assembly a new role in the maintenance of peace and security. In case of a veto in the Security Council, the General Assembly could be convened within twenty-four hours and make recommendations for collective measures, including the use of armed forces, in cases of breaches of the peace or acts of aggression. The resolution was adopted by thirty-nine votes to five, which reveals the extent of American dominance in the Assembly at the time.

The Soviet government denounced these new procedures as a violation of one of the fundamental principles of the Charter, under which decisions on the use of armed force by the UN could only be made by the Security Council with the consent, or at least the acquiescence, of all the five permanent members. If such decisions could be made by majority vote in the General Assembly over the opposition of a permanent member, the UN could be turned into an alliance led by one big power against another.

Throughout the negotiations on the Charter, Stalin had insisted on retaining the right of veto as an indispensable condition for Soviet participation in the postwar organization. Not surprisingly, Soviet protests against the "Uniting for Peace" resolution were vitriolic. But why did the Soviet Union not withdraw from the UN altogether? Was it simply because of the general immobilism of Soviet policy in Stalin's last years? Or was the decision not to leave the UN based on a far-sighted calculation of future changes in the balance of forces? Whatever the reasons, the Soviets stayed on, stolidly accepting defeat in one vote after another. The Soviet ambassador at the time, Yakov Malik, later proudly recalled he had cast over forty vetos "in defense of socialism," as he put it. And soon enough the great wheel of world politics turned once again full circle, depositing the United States and the Soviet Union on the same side in a Third World conflict.

It is indeed one of the many ironies of the history of the UN that the one time the "Uniting for Peace" resolution was employed with practical effect it was used to circumvent a veto cast in the Security Council, not by the Soviet Union, but by America's two closest allies, Britain and France. This was in the Suez crisis in October–November 1956. As Israeli tanks were advancing across Sinai, and British and

French forces were preparing to invade the Suez Canal Zone, the Security Council met on October 29 to consider a United States resolution calling upon Israel to withdraw its forces from Egypt and asking all member states — in effect Britain and France — to refrain from the use or threat of force. The Soviet Union voted yes, but Britain and France cast their veto to prevent the Security Council from making a decision. Two days later the Security Council, invoking the "Uniting for Peace" procedure, decided to call an emergency session of the General Assembly, and the Soviet Union, in spite of its strong objections to what it considered a perversion of Charter principles, supported the move. Not letting principle stand in the way of political advantage is politely called pragmatism: an "ism" more powerful than Communism.

This display of American-Soviet anticolonial solidarity in the UN masked the beginning of a thirty year war between the two powers for dominance in the Third World. By stopping the Anglo-French Suez expedition, the United States was actually preventing an extension of Soviet influence, or so the American policymakers believed. As President Eisenhower put it, "We could not permit the Soviet Union to seize the leadership in the struggle against the use of force in the Middle East and thus win the confidence of the new independent nations of the world."[6] The Soviet government, on its part, was prepared to be pragmatic about UN procedures in order to prove its loyalty to the Arabs in their fight against British and French imperialism.

For the UN, the Suez crisis had far-reaching consequences. One was the birth of what we today call peacekeeping; another, the enhanced role of the Secretary-General as an independent actor on the world scene. These added a new dimension to the capacity of the UN to serve member states in crises and conflicts, but very soon they also plunged the UN itself into a deep crisis that shook its very foundations.

The idea of using a UN force in Suez was first publicly launched by Lester Pearson, foreign minister of Canada, but it would be more accurate to say that it was born out of the creative confusion that reigned in the UN during the tense days and nights of early November 1956. Washington feared that Moscow might send "volunteers" to the Middle East or stop the flow of oil to the West, in order to save Nasser from defeat. The stage was set for a major confrontation. It was one thing to pass a resolution urging a cease-fire and a withdrawal of all forces; another, as Pearson pointed out, to persuade all the parties to comply with it. His solution was designed to help Britain and France save face by allowing them to hand over the Canal Zone to a UN force rather than to the Egyptians themselves.

Secretary-General Dag Hammarskjöld was not immediately receptive to Pearson's idea, but the United States was and pressed on with urgency. Henry Cabot Lodge, then US representative to the UN, told me once how it happened. He received from the State Department the draft of a resolution requesting the Secretary General to submit within forty-eight hours a plan for an emergency UN force, but he was instructed to have someone else submit it to the General Assembly. As he walked across First Avenue from the US Mission to the UN building he decided to ask either Lester Pearson or Henri-Paul Spaak, the Belgian foreign minister, who ever he ran into first, to sponsor the resolution. It happened to be Pearson, and so it was that Pearson was awarded the Nobel Peace Prize as the father of peacekeeping.

The plàn Hammarskjöld and his team produced in forty-eight hours as requested represented a genuine innovation in international diplomacy and set out the principles and procedures that were to become a model for future UN peacekeeping operations. The UN Emergency Force (UNEF) was a complex and subtle construction — an instrument of diplomacy disguised as a military force. It had a military field commander, a Canadian general, but political control was placed firmly in the hands of the Secretary-General. Its deployment on Egyptian territory required the consent of the Egyptian government, and it was composed of military units from neutral and other countries acceptable to the Egyptian government. The five permanent members of the Security Council were excluded. UNEF was not permitted to use force except in self-defense. Its function was symbolic, not military. Its initial task was to ease the departure of the Anglo-French force from the Suez Canal Zone, but after the withdrawal of the Israeli forces from Sinai UNEF was deployed in 1957 along the armistice line on the Egyptian side where for the next ten years it provided Nasser with an alibi for not attacking Israel.

The Soviets objected to the establishment of UNEF on the grounds that it violated the Charter. The Soviets read the Charter the way fundamentalists read the Bible. The Charter makes no mention of peacekeeping operations; it follows that such operations are illegal. According to the Charter only the Security Council is empowered to decide on the use of armed force; a force established by a decision of the General Assembly must therefore be unconstitutional. The Charter stipulates that the Military Staff Committee must direct a UN military operation; it was therefore wrong to place UNEF under the direction of the Secretary-General. What the Soviet Union really objected to was the fact that UNEF operated outside of the reach of the Soviet veto. Consequently the Soviet Union did not vote for the General Assembly resolution establishing UNEF nor would it make a voluntary contribution to the fund set up to finance the operation. Yet the Soviet Union refrained from actually opposing the UN intervention in Suez, because it was designed to get the Anglo-French force out of there and to save Nasser from humiliation and thus served Soviet interests. Hammarskjöld, too, was judged by Moscow by what he did rather than by what he said, as long as his actions did not go against Soviet interests.

Deus ex Machina

In the Suez war there were no victors, but in the theater of world politics a star was born. The crisis provided Dag Hammarskjöld, the Swedish diplomat who had been appointed Secretary-General in April 1953, with an opportunity to demonstrate his superior intellectual capacity, resourcefulness, and presence of mind under great pressure. President Eisenhower complimented him publicly; his prestige soared. More important, he acquired in peacekeeping a tool which enabled him to exercise an independent influence in conflict situations. He used it in a variety of ways — for instance, by sending observers to Lebanon and by establishing a "UN presence" in Laos.

On the occasion of his reappointment to a second term in 1957, Hammarskjöld was ready to put forward the view "that it was in keeping with the philosophy of the Charter that the Secretary-General should be expected to act also without guidance found in the Charter, or in the decisions of the main organs of the United Nations, should this appear to him to be necessary in order to help in filling any vacuum that may appear in the systems that the Charter and traditional diplomacy provide for the safeguarding of peace and security."[7] This was a revolutionary concept granting the Secretary-General an open-ended mandate to take independent action. Yet at the time it went unchallenged. Perhaps Hammarskjöld's baroque prose style helped to obscure what he really meant. At any rate governments do not normally engage in debate on a philosophical plane. They react to events, not to ideas; they are guided by interests, not principles.

Hammarskjöld himself was aware, however, that the course he had chosen might lead "into the storm." Indeed, he deliberately steered the UN toward it. When the Belgian colony of the Congo acceded to independence in June 1960 and immediately was plunged into chaos, Hammarskjöld virtually solicited from the Congolese leaders a request for UN assistance and called on his own initiative a meeting of the Security Council to authorize him to dispatch a peacekeeping force to the newly born African state. "You try to save a drowning man," he later explained, "without prior authorization or even if he resists you."

Hammarskjöld took upon himself the role of a benevolent and disinterested godfather to the peoples emerging from colonial rule: by helping them in the task of nation-building the UN could protect them from being sucked into the Cold War. The choice in the Congo, in his view, was between assistance from the UN and dependence upon one or other of the superpowers. It was a decisive moment, he said, "not only for the future of the UN but also for the future of Africa. And Africa may well in present circumstances mean the world."[8]

In hindsight, Hammarskjöld's statement sounds like hyperbole, but his view of the significance of the Congo crisis was widely shared at the time. The power of Russia, Walter Lippman wrote after a meeting with Soviet Leader Nikita Khrushchev in October 1957, lay "in the force of its example" upon the developing states of Africa, Asia and Latin America. The West could counter that example only by demonstrating that it was possible to improve the condition of backward societies without sacrificing democracy. The Russians, according to Lippman, were convinced they could win that contest, but that the United States would resort to war to prevent them from winning.[9] Neither side had forgotten Lenin's prediction that the revolution would reach London and Paris by way of Asia and Africa. The impact of the emerging states of the Third World was specially strong in the UN: In 1960, seating in the Assembly hall had to be rearranged to accommodate the delegations from sixteen new African member states.

In this atmosphere, a tribal power struggle in one of the most backward areas of Africa was blown up into a world crisis, with the UN — and Hammarskjöld personally — at its center. The Congo (now Zaire) became the scene of the largest and most complex peacekeeping operation ever mounted by the UN. Lasting four years and costing more than 400 million dollars, at one point it included almost 20,000 troops. In addition, a substantial program of technical and economic assistance was administered by the UN. The Congo operation also produced a spate of lively and controversial books through which the literate intellectuals sent there by the UN as its representatives went on fighting each other for years after the operation had come to an end.

Initially, the United States and the Soviet Union once again, as in the Suez crisis, found themselves united in an anticolonial spirit, supporting Hammarskjöld's proposal for a UN intervention, while Britain and France abstained. But the Congo war was fought simultaneously on two fronts: one between the African state struggling to be born and its former colonial masters; the other, between Western and Soviet political influence. On the former front, the decisive issue was the future of Katanga, the wealthiest province of the Congo, which under its leader Moise Tshombe, aided by Belgian, French, British and American business interests, declared its intention to secede and establish a separate state. One of the principal aims of the UN operation was to restore the unity of the Congo, and in this Hammarskjöld had the support of the Soviet Union. But when the pro-Soviet side in the Congolese power struggle was defeated and Patrice Lumumba, Moscow's protégé, was killed, the Soviet government turned against the Secretary-General. It did not help him that he could point to the support of India and key African states, or to the hostility of France, Belgium and Britain, as evidence of the impartiality of his actions.

It was a mistake to imagine that the governments of the big powers would judge him by some abstract or objective criteria. Khrushchev was not likely to say: "This time Hammarskjöld went against us, but it is only fair, last time he was with us." He judged Hammarskjöld by the immediate political consequences of his actions, in each concrete case separately. "Objectively", as the Soviets put it, the UN operation in the Congo served the interests of the United States, indeed, this is how it was seen in Washington, too. President Kennedy, like Eisenhower before him, was convinced that "if we didn't have the UN operation, the only way to block Soviet domination in the Congo would be to go in with our own forces."[10] Accordingly the United States was prepared to pay close to half the costs of the peacekeeping operation and more than half the civilian assistance program, while the Soviet Union refused to pay a penny. For the United States it was enough to make sure the Congo would not fall under Soviet domination; for Moscow any outcome other than a victory for the revolution meant defeat. This lack of symmetry between the interests of the two superpowers snared Hammarskjöld in a fatal trap. There was no way he could conduct the Congo operation, given its purpose of protecting the country from the cold war, without running into a head-on collision with the Soviet Union. As a result his capacity to act successfully as Secretary-General was destroyed. And on September 18, 1961, he met his death in a plane crash on his way from the Congo to a meeting with Tshombe in Rhodesia.

The UN operation in the Congo went on for three more years. Katanga was brought to heel by the UN forces acting "in self-defense." The leader who emerged out of the chaos was a young military man by name of Joseph Mobutu, neither a communist nor a democrat, who has ruled ever since over the Republic of Zaire. Like several of his colleagues in other African states Mobutu has amassed a huge personal fortune; unlike most others, he has managed to keep his country out of the news. His gift to his people has been a reasonable measure of political stability — not a negligible achievement by African standards. Perhaps it calls for two cheers for the UN effort. But it is no longer terribly important; the Congo crisis hardly merits more than a footnote in the history of the cold war.

In the history of the UN, however, the Congo operation was a watershed event. For a few moments in history Hammarskjöld had succeeded in making the UN — that is, the office of the Secretary-General — an autonomous influence in international politics, representing, in his words, "the detached element in international life." He had seen himself as an ombudsman of the small nations, entitled "to voice

the wishes of the peoples against this or that government."[11] His goal
was to transform the UN from a static conference machinery for
resolving conflicts of interests into a dynamic instrument of the
collective responsibility of the membership — a heroic effort doomed
to failure. The major powers were prepared to support him only so long
as both sides in the cold war could benefit from what he did. They
would not tolerate a policy equally damaging to both. Hammarskjöld's
notion that the very fact of membership in the UN placed limits on the
national ambitions of states was rejected not only by the Soviet Union
but also by the United States and especially by General de Gaulle,
whose disdain for the UN was more devastating than anything said by
Ronald Reagan twenty years later. Nonetheless, Washington continued
to support Dag Hammarskjöld and, after his death, the idea of an
independent Secretary-General. It did so because at the time the
independence of the Secretary-General was believed to be useful to the
United States as a counterweight to the Soviet veto. As circumstances
changed, the United States lost interest in the concept. But the myth
created by Hammarskjöld's virtuoso performance lived on. It acquired
a mystic dimension by the publication after his death of his diary, which
revealed his Messianic sense of mission, and the yearning shared by
many for an impartial authority standing above the narrow rivalries
between national governments, a deus ex machina ready to resolve
conflicts in a spirit of rationality and fairness.

Yet Hammarskjöld's legacy, in political terms, was ambiguous.
At the height of Congo crisis he wrote to a friend: "I have had to
choose between the risk that the Organization would break down and
die out of inertia and inability and the risk that it might break up and
die because I have overstretched its possibilities."[12] In the end, the
challenge posed by Hammarskjöld's dynamic concept of his role did
bring the UN to the very brink of a breakdown.

Détente UN Style

The post-Hammarskjöld crisis was ostensibly about money, but in reality
about power. The refusal of the Soviet Union and France to pay for
peacekeeping operations they regarded as unconstitutional was a protest
directed at the United States as the power that had engineered the
Uniting for Peace procedure making it possible to transfer to the

General Assembly part of the authority which under the Charter belonged exclusively to the Security Council. The immediate target, however, was the office of the Secretary-General.

Hammarskjöld had established the practice by which the Secretary-General, having received either from the Security Council or the General Assembly a general mandate for mounting a peacekeeping operation, negotiated the necessary agreements with the states involved, determined the composition of the UN force, appointed its commander, and issued the political instructions for the conduct of the operation. In the Soviet and French view,the Congo operation had shown that even with a mandate from the Security Council, a peacekeeping operation could be directed by the Secretary General in a manner inconsistent with the intentions of one or two of the permanent members. For this reason, it was argued, the Council itself had to retain detailed control of any operation.

Soviet leader Nikita Khrushchev went so far as to suggest that "the post of Secretary-General who alone directs the staff and alone interprets and executes the decisions of the Security Council and the General Assembly should be abolished." His "troika" alternative was that the executive organ of the UN should consist of three persons, representing respectively the military bloc of the Western powers, the socialist states, and the neutral countries. Such an arrangement was designed to make sure that the day-to-day management of the UN would at all times be subject to the veto.

Khrushchev's "troika" was a nonstarter. It never received much support, even among the nonaligned states. But as a tactical move it served the Soviets well. In the aftermath of Hammarskjöld's death the West was impelled by the fear of the troika to look for a successor whom the Soviet Union could not possibly refuse. They found U Thant, a Burmese diplomat, who represented the nonaligned world which both the West and the Soviet Union were eagerly courting. His election was considered a defeat for the Soviet Union: The troika was never mentioned again. But the Soviets grew very fond of U Thant. He turned out to be a one-man troika.

Unlike Hammarskjöld who was an inscrutable Scandinavian,

U Thant was a very straightforward Oriental, a sphinx without a secret. He liked to call himself "moderator," a term once used by President Roosevelt to describe the function of the Secretary-General. "I have always felt that the most important political duty of the Secretary-General was to concentrate on the harmonizing functions of the UN," U Thant once said. "I have been at pains to understand and to remain on cooperative terms with all the governments."[13] This philosophy stood in sharp contrast to that of his predecessor who had declared that he would "rather see the office of the Secretary-General break on strict adherence to the principle of independence, impartiality and objectivity than drift on the basis of compromise."[14]

But U Thant was determined not to be another Hammarskjöld. His overriding purpose was to save the UN from breaking up at the time, the only line to take. The constitutional conflict that had arisen between the major powers had put the very existence of the Organization at risk. The Secretary-General's first duty had to be to restore unity.

The full implications of U Thant's concept of his role did not become immediately apparent. Lacking the intellectual capacity or political sophistication of his predecessor, U Thant was heavily dependent on his senior advisers in the Secretariat, most of whom had worked closely with Hammarskjöld and were committed to carrying on in his tradition. Peacekeeping operations remained in the hands of Ralph Bunche, the American Undersecretary-General, and his deputy Brian Urquhart, a British national; both had served in the UN from the very beginning and were totally devoted to the ideal of an independent international civil service. They continued the practice established by Hammarskjöld which was designed to exclude the Soviet Union and its allies from participation in peacekeeping operations. The chain of command bypassed the Soviet citizens in the Secretariat, and in the field no personnel of the Soviet Union or its allies were ever used. The argument for such a procedure was that, since the Soviet Union was opposed in principle to the very concept of peacekeeping, nationals of Soviet bloc countries could not be trusted to serve loyally in such operations. In this manner the Congo operation was continued under U Thant, and in 1964 the peacekeeping operation in Cyprus was mounted under the command of the Secretary-General, despite objections from the Soviet Union and France. Throughout U Thant's first term (1961–66) a facade of continuity was maintained.

But once again, as in 1956, a crisis in the Middle East became a turning point for the UN and its Secretary-General, though this time no star was born. In May 1967 President Nasser demanded that the UN Emergency Force be withdrawn from the Sinai, and U Thant promptly agreed to do so.

The decision provoked a storm of criticism in the West. Much of it was uninformed and unfair. UNEF was not a force of occupation. Its presence on Egyptian soil was based on the consent of the Egyptian government. Since Israel refused to allow it to operate on her side of the armistice line, UNEF was wholly dependent on the cooperation of the Egyptian authorities. It was no fighting force, and none of the governments which had placed troops at the disposal of the UN was prepared to risk the lives of its soldiers. Indeed, India and Yugoslavia announced they would withdraw their contingents in any case, regardless of what U Thant might decide. The Secretary-General could claim he had no choice but to comply with Nasser's request.

Nevertheless questions linger. Why did U Thant not refer the matter to the Security Council on the ground that Nasser's request created a situation likely to endanger international peace and security? Article 99 of the Charter authorizes the Secretary-General to draw the attention of the Security Council to such a situation. His answer was that the Security Council at the time was hopelessly divided on the Middle East issue. "Nothing could be more divisive and useless", he said later, "than for the Secretary-General to bring a situation publicly to the Security Council when there was no practical possibility of the Council's agreeing on effective or useful action."[15]

This was the official explanation. But privately U Thant told me at the time that he had to consider how his own position might be affected by taking the issue to the Security Council. Western representatives were urging the UN to take steps to prevent war, while Soviet and Arab spokesmen dismissed such warnings as alarmist and irresponsible. Had the Secretary-General claimed that Nasser's request for the withdrawal of UNEF was likely to endanger international peace and security he would have injected himself into an acute controversy between East and West. Without doubt he would have been accused of partisanship; he might have run the risk of an irreparable break with the Soviet Union. "I would have lost my future usefulness as Secretary-General, like Hammarskjöld," U Thant said to me.

His arguments cannot be dismissed simply as cowardly or self-serving. As anyone who was there at the time can testify, the Security Council was hopelessly deadlocked. A personal intervention by the Secretary-General would have been no more than a heroic gesture: it could not have resulted in meaningful action. Any attempt to bring pressure on Nasser would have been blocked, not only by the Soviet Union, but above all by the nonaligned group. For this reason U Thant's room for manoeuver was virtually non-existent. Hammarskjöld had been able to operate in the Congo crisis against Soviet opposition with the support of India and key African states; in the Middle East crisis in 1967 the nonaligned group — U Thant's personal constituency — solidly backed the demand for a withdrawal of UNEF. "My conception of the UN was primarily from the vantage point of view of the Third World," he later wrote.[16]

In the West, the image of U Thant as an independent actor on the world stage was shattered by the events of May and June 1967. But though the United States and the Soviet Union continued to quarrel over the authority of the Secretary-General in peacekeeping operations, the issue was no longer as important as it had appeared previously. By 1967 American-Soviet relations had moved a long way toward what later became known as détente. The power vacuum which Hammarskjöld had tried to fill with his personal diplomacy no longer existed.

The Goldberg Era

The beginning of the change can be pinpointed with unusual precision. It was in the summer of 1965. The Organization was virtually paralyzed by the dispute about the financing of peacekeeping operations. Article 19 of the Charter provides that a member state which is in arrears for an amount equal to or greater than contributions due for the pre-ceeding two years shall be deprived of its vote in the General Assembly. In the fall of 1964 the money owed by the Soviet Union and its allies exceeded the critical limit; in the beginning of 1965 France was added to the list of delinquents. The governments of these states argued that contributions for the peacekeeping operations in the Congo and the Middle East were not mandatory because these operations were not in accordance with the Charter. But the International Court of Justice stated in a majority opinion that the money spent on peacekeeping operations authorized by the General Assembly did constitute regular expenses of the Organization that had to be shared by all member states, and the Court's opinion was accepted by the General Assembly by a vote of seventy-six to seventeen, with eight abstentions.

The conclusion seemed inevitable. Yet many of the governments that had voted for the Court opinion lacked the courage of their convictions. It was one thing to vote for the principle involved, quite another to blackball two major powers. Soviet diplomats were hinting that their country, if deprived the right to vote, would withdraw from the UN altogether. Against this threat the American insistence on defending the authority of the General Assembly on financial issues sounded like a demand to "let justice be done though the world perish."

Torn between the need to uphold the principles of the Charter and the realities of power, the General Assembly had gone through all sorts of procedural contortions in order to put off the moment of truth. At the end of its 1964 session it had even voted to decide whether or not voting was permissible, thus resorting to farce in order to avoid tragedy. But by summer 1965 all possibilities of evasion seemed to have been exhausted. The Assembly session due to begin in September would have to face the awful choice between abdicating its financial authority and risking a walk-out by the delegates of two permanent members of the Security Council.

These events of May 1965 coincided with my arrival at the UN as permanent representative of Finland. One of the first persons I called on was Adlai Stevenson. In European eyes his stature as a spokesman for America was second only to the President himself, and I looked forward to receiving authoritative answers to the many troubled questions discussed among delegates at the time. But Stevenson seemed curiously distracted and vague. I had to go to one of his aides to get a briefing on the American position on the financial crisis. I left with the disturbing impression that American policy was stuck in a groove and the UN was drifting, leaderless, towards disaster.

A few weeks later, in July, came the news of Adlai Stevenson's death. For once the UN was undivided in its shock and grief. The crisis stood still. Nothing could be done before the United States President had filled the void left by Adlai Stevenson.

President Lyndon Johnson's choice of Arthur Goldberg carried a message the UN community at first failed to understand. Arthur Goldberg, a Justice of the Supreme Court and former Secretary of Labor in the Kennedy administration, had no record in foreign relations. Most of us were puzzled by why he had been chosen, and why he had agreed to abandon the prestige and security of his Supreme Court seat in order to serve as captain of a sinking ship. The reason became apparent only later — Johnson's promise to give him a key role in the search of a negotiated peace in Vietnam. This was an offer no American with a sense of responsibility could refuse.

Goldberg arrived at the UN with the kind of backing from the White House that Stevenson had been denied. This may have been one reason why he was resented by many of those who had loved and admired Stevenson. They considered him crude and pompous; worse, a lousy speaker. But public speeches at the UN are for the American gallery; their impact on the UN process itself is negligible. Besides, one can never tell what is left of a witty or elegant phrase after it has passed through simultaneous translation. The real influence of the US Mission depends on a mix of private negotiations, parliamentary maneuvers and discreet lobbying in the capitals of member states. As an experienced negotiator, Goldberg quickly mastered the instruments of persuasion and pressure at his disposal. It did not take him long to acquire a commanding position of leadership in the UN. The first thing he did was to persuade Washington to accept the fact that the General Assembly would not apply sanctions against the Soviet Union and France. In a statement on August 16, 1965, Goldberg announced that the United States would not demand a vote on the constitutional issue. He added, however, that "if any member can insist on making an exception to the principle of collective financial responsibility with respect to certain activities of the Organization, the United States reserves the same option . . . There can be no double standard among the members."[17] Fifteen years later the United States did begin to exercise this option — with a vengeance. As a result the financial crisis of the UN is worse now than in the post-Hammarskjöld period.

The American retreat on the constitutional issue has been called the end of an era: the end of American hegemony within the UN. As membership had risen to 118, the United States could no longer rely on a pro-American majority. Goldberg and his team had counted the votes and come to the conclusion that a battle over Article 19 would end in defeat. But he must have also considered that it might result in victory — a much greater disaster. A victory would have ruined Goldberg's mission, which was to work for a negotiated peace in Vietnam, which could not be achieved without the cooperation of the Soviet Union. It would have made no sense to cause a rupture with Moscow and possibly destroy the usefulness of the UN for the sake of defending the authority of a General Assembly which no longer could be relied upon to serve the interests of the United States. The retreat on Article 19 meant, in effect, that United States policy in the UN finally caught up with the policy of détente Washington had initiated a couple of years earlier.

It did not mean, however, that the Vietnam issue itself could be dealt with in the UN. Goldberg soon found out that, while every speaker in the general debate at each Assembly session had something to say about the war in Vietnam, hardly anyone was actually prepared to discuss ways and means of settling the conflict. The formal reason for keeping Vietnam off the UN agenda was that neither North Vietnam nor South Vietnam was a member of the Organization and that Communist China was not represented. The real reason was quite different. The leaders of North Vietnam rejected the competence of the UN to deal with the war, because in their view it was not a war between two states but an internal struggle for the unification of the Vietnamese nation. And as long as Hanoi said no, its supporters in the UN opposed every attempt to consider the issue in New York.

In January 1966 Goldberg did manage to persuade the required majority — nine out of the fifteen members of Security Council — to vote for a proposal to inscribe the Vietnam war on the agenda, but the ninth vote — Japan — was conditioned on the understanding that the Council would not actually meet on this issue until further consultations indicated that a meeting would be fruitful, and this never happened.[18] The allies and friends of the United States were relieved not to be confronted with the embarrassing choice between offending the Americans and facing criticism at home.

The inability of the UN to deal with the one issue that at the time overshadowed all other on the world scene created the kind of "vacuum at the heart of the international system" that Hammarskjöld had described as a legitimate field for independent action on the part of the SecretaryGeneral. U Thant did try his hand at personal diplomacy, but his efforts in late 1964 and early 1965 to arrange meetings between representatives of the United States and Hanoi were rebuffed by Washington. The problem was not lack of contact or any misunderstanding between the parties. The parties understood each other only too well: Hanoi was bent upon unifying Vietnam under its leadership, while the United States was determined to defend its ally, South Vietnam. No compromise was possible so long as each side was confident it could succeed. But U Thant was deeply hurt by the dismissive manner with which President Johnson and Secretary of State Dean Rusk treated his initiatives, and disappointed when Peking, too, rejected his offer of mediation and called him a running dog of the superpowers. He even announced he would refuse to accept reappointment as Secretary-General at the end of his term November 1966. This was taken to mean that he had lost confidence in America's desire for peace. What followed was an odd piece of political theatre put on for the benefit of the American public. The Soviet Union and France, which supported U Thant and agreed with his criticism of United States policy in Vietnam, pretended to take his threat seriously and made no attempt in public to persuade him to continue, while Goldberg pleaded with him to agree to accept a second term. In the end, of course, U Thant accepted, and everyone was satisfied.[19]

Though the UN was not the place where the Vietnam conflict could be resolved, Vietnam did not prevent the United States and the Soviet Union from drawing closer on other issues in the UN. Indeed, Vietnam helped the two powers to set aside their differences and find ways to cooperate.

The Cuban crisis gave the first impulse to the policy of détente. Having drawn back from the brink of a nuclear war, the governments of the United States and the Soviet Union began their search for means to bring the nuclear arms race under control. This was the main road of détente. The evolution of American-Soviet cooperation in the UN in the latter part of the 1960s and beginning of the 1970s was a side road. The Vietnam war provided a powerful impetus. American policymakers believed Mao's China to be the evil power behind Hanoi's ambitions; the Soviet leaders were obsessed with what they perceived to be the mortal threat posed by the combination of Maoist doctrine and Chinese nationalist aspirations. "The enemy of my enemy is my friend," is a maxim that has produced many reversals of alliances in the course of history.

The new power constellation became visible in August 1965, when large-scale hostilities broke out between India and Pakistan. Both superpowers wanted to prevent the war from spreading, and quickly agreed in the Security Council on a cease-fire resolution. But China encouraged Pakistan not to give in, and the fighting went on. The United States and the Soviet Union then withheld military and economic aid from both parties, which finally persuaded them to accept a cease-fire under UN supervision.

What would have had happened if the seat of China in the Security Council had been held by the representatives of Mao's government? I remember Secretary of State Dean Rusk asking the question at the time. Of course China would have vetoed any attempt by the Council to bring about a peaceful settlement. Rusk used this as an argument in favour of keeping Peking out of the UN. He thus implicitly recognized the Soviet Union as a constructive partner interested in peaceful solutions. Peking on its part denounced what it called a conspiracy between imperialist America and "social-imperialist" Russia to rule the world. Peking's spokesman in the UN at the time was the representative of Albania, a lonely dissident shunned by the delegations of the other socialist countries and dismissed by his Western colleagues as an odd eccentric. Yet he was worth listening to, for through him spoke to us the mad ruler of one quarter of mankind.

After the India-Pakistan war came the Arab-Israel war: once again, though this time only after a great deal of pain and confusion, the United States and the Soviet Union reached agreement on the need for a cease-fire under UN supervision. And a much more important step followed. In November 1967 the Security Council unanimously adopted Resolution 242 which provided the framework for a comprehensive settlement of the Middle East conflict. This was the first time the Security Council, in consultation with the parties involved, worked out and adopted a plan designed to achieve a solution of a major international conflict to be carried out under UN auspices and by the use of a UN mediator and other UN services. (A detailed analysis of this event belongs to the chapter dealing with the Middle East.) I mention it here as a product of détente. Resolution 242 was an embryo of an American-Soviet partnership for the purpose of containing and eliminating regional conflicts. From the American point of view détente was a policy designed to neutralize the Soviet Union in the Vietnam war or, better still, to obtain Soviet help in the effort to reach "peace with honor." Moscow had more far-reaching goals. It hoped to neutralize the United States in a possible future conflict with China or, still better, draw it into an anti-Chinese alliance.

Non-Proliferation

China's first nuclear test in October 1964 was taken in Moscow as a warning that time was short. The Soviet hawks were anxious to take action before China could acquire a nuclear arsenal. But first the European situation had to be consolidated. In January 1965 the Warsaw Pact launched its proposal for the convening of a European security conference. This was an old Soviet idea. In 1954 Molotov had proposed a similar conference with a view to preventing the inclusion of West Germany into the Western alliance. He had proposed a neutralized united Germany, a concept rejected out of hand by the Western allies. Now, in 1965, the German issue was still the heart of the matter. But Moscow no longer talked of a unified Germany. The purpose of the proposed security conference was rather to confirm the permanence of the division of Germany.

According to the Soviet plan, security in Europe required "respect for the European realities" — an euphemism for the existing power structure in Eastern Europe. In more concrete terms, it demanded acceptance of the borders established at the end of the second world war, recognition of two separate sovereign German states, and safeguards against West Germany obtaining access to nuclear weapons.

In a formal sense the Soviet program appeared irreconcilable with the prevailing Western position. The West was still committed to supporting the goal of German unification. The official Western view was that the Federal Republic of Germany was entitled to speak for the whole of German nation, the Democratic Republic of Germany was a Soviet puppet regime without legitimate claim to international recognition, and the German borders were provisional until confirmed by a peace treaty. As for nuclear weapons, West Germany was to have access to them within the safe context of a multilateral fleet (MLF).

In fact, however, the Soviet design for Europe was much closer to what people in the West really wanted than the policy their governments pretended to support. As Francois Mauriac, the French writer, once pointed out, the French love Germany so much that they prefer to have two of them. The same was true of the other Western neighbors of Germany. There was no genuine support for the goal of a German unification, no interest in reopening the issue of the eastern border of Germany and no readiness to risk war for the sake of challenging the "European realities." And the abortive talks on the MLF project revealed how reluctant the European allies were to allow a German finger on the nuclear trigger. Moscow clearly had a winning ticket.

Points one and two on the Soviet program — recognition of two German states and acceptance of the borders — were dealt with initially in bilateral negotiations with the Federal Republic of Germany under the heading of Willy Brandt's Ostpolitik. They were the kind of "transitional security arrangements" excluded from the UN agenda. But point three — denial of nuclear weapons to Germany — had to be dealt with in the wider context of a general treaty to prevent the spread of nuclear weapons.

Such a treaty had been proposed in the UN by Foreign Minister Frank Aiken of Ireland as early as in 1959, but it was only in the mid-1960s that the nuclear powers themselves begun to take a real interest. The Chinese nuclear test was a warning signal. It was too late to prevent China from becoming a nuclear power, but it was all the more urgent to draw the line there. If even one or two countries followed the Chinese example, how could the Germans be stopped? In more general terms, it was essential to prevent a proliferation of nuclear weapons before the two superpowers could start reducing their strategic arsenals and agree on a limitation of anti-ballistic missile defenses.

On October 7, 1966, President Johnson made a speech that signalled an important reversal of American policy with regard to Germany and East-West relations in general. Until that time the United States had considered a solution of the German question a precondition of an improvement between East and West. Now Johnson declared that an improvement in East-West relations must precede progress in the German question. Four days later it was announced that the United States and the Soviet Union had initiated high level talks on a non-proliferation treaty. This was followed in January 1967 by an agreement in principle to begin discussions on limiting strategic arms.

The Non-Proliferation Treaty (NPT) negotiations lasted throughout 1967. In January 1968 the treaty was ready for submission to a special session of the UN General Assembly which opened in April. For the first time since the end of the Second World War the two superpowers presented to the Assembly a joint proposal of far-reaching importance. This was a unique accomplishment. For once the UN was not just reacting to events but was initiating constructive action to limit the risk of future conflicts by building a global legal regime designed to prevent the spread of nuclear weapons.[20]

According to the American-Soviet treaty, the states which possessed nuclear weapons were to pledge not to transfer them "to any recipient whatsoever" and not in any way to "assist, encourage, or induce" any state to manufacture or acquire such weapons. The states which did not possess nuclear weapons pledged not to receive or to manufacture them or receive assistance in their manufacture. The self-imposed denial of the non-nuclear weapon states was to be matched, ultimately, by corresponding acts by the nuclear powers to pursue negotiations in "good faith" to halt the nuclear arms race "at an early date" and to bring about nuclear disarmament.

The treaty thus went to the heart of the strategy of the great powers and the security of all states. It affected the sensitive political relationships within the alliances as well as between them. The prestige and pride of nations was at stake. The overwhelming majority of the states of the world were requested to give up forever the option of acquiring the most powerful weapons yet invented, while recognizing the right of five states — Roosevelt's Five Policemen — to retain such weapons in their arsenals.

The United States and the Soviet Union were equally anxious to obtain for their treaty as wide an endorsement as possible. Their joint campaign in the General Assembly was headed on the American side by Arthur Goldberg, while Moscow sent its chief trouble-shooter, Deputy Foreign Minister Vasiliy Kuznetsov. His arrival on the scene meant the Kremlin was ready to get down to serious bargaining. Kuznetsov had negotiated the removal of the Soviet missiles from Cuba and Security Council Resolution 242. (Later he was to be sent to Prague in 1968 and to Peking in 1969.) Having studied engineering in Pittsburgh and worked in the Ford plant in Detroit in the 1930s, Kuznetsov spoke English well: he personified what the Russians mean by the term "business-like."

Goldberg and Kuznetsov needed a shock absorber to cushion the impact of superpower dictation to a resentful General Assembly. I was that cushion. They asked me as representative of neutral Finland to convene a group of delegations to act as sponsors of the NPT resolution. They knew my government strongly supported the treaty, since Finland had signed away her own nuclear option in the peace treaty of 1946. Finland also believed the NPT would contribute to a lessening of East-West tensions in Europe by allaying Russian fears of a resurgence of German military power, and Finland only stood to gain from such a development. Besides, it was in the Finnish interest to render the two superpowers the kind of services they asked for: by making itself useful to both sides a neutral country reinforces its own neutrality.

Acting as campaign manager for the two superpowers proved to be a strange experience. Since the text of the NPT had been approved on the highest level in both capitals, not a comma could be changed without a cumbersome process of renegotiation. No detail was too insignificant to warrant the personal attention of Goldberg and Kuznetsov, neither of whom took a single step without being accompanied by at least five high-level advisors. I felt at times like a little boy in charge of two elephants.

It was not easy to recruit sponsors for the NPT. There were defections even from the ranks of the two alliances and the European neutrals. None of the Latin American or African countries showed up. Yet almost everyone was prepared to agree in principle with the proposition that the acquisition of nuclear weapons would not add to the security of a nation; on the contrary, it would tend to increase its risks. A report prepared by a group of experts stated that nuclear weapons "might bring with it the penalty of becoming a direct target for nuclear attacks." In fact, very few of the states which refused the sponsorship had ever thought of acquiring nuclear weapons for themselves. Most of them were simply demonstrating against being bullied by the big powers. The irony of it was that for years these same countries had urged the big powers to bury their differences. Now that the two begun to cooperate they were accused of creating a superpower condominium.

Peking denounced the NPT, claiming it revealed the existence of an unholy alliance between the United States and the Soviet Union established to suppress the national liberation movements and the independence of peace-loving peoples. Even the government of neutral Sweden had its misgivings. "Détente is not without risks for small states," the late Prime Minister Olof Palme pointed out. "In the name of détente the superpowers may resist any change to the point of permitting the continuation of an unjust or dangerous situation." The Swedes, among many others, complained that the nuclear powers had failed to offer convincing guarantees that they would actually begin to reduce their own nuclear arsenals. If nuclear weapons posed such a mortal danger to international security, why should one begin with eliminating hypothetical nuclear weapons which may or may not be produced in the future, while leaving the existing weapons in place? The skeptics were quite right in doubting the "good faith" of the superpowers: ratification of the NPT was followed by a nuclear arms race that lasted for twenty years and reached proportions none of us could have imagined.

The NPT debate, like many UN debates then and now, was mostly about what the world should be like, rather than what it really is like. No one referred to Germany, though from the Soviet point of view, as Kuznetsov frankly told me, the whole point of the exercise was to make sure that West Germany would renounce nuclear weapons. Very few speakers said anything about China. Yet China was very much on the minds of both the Russians and the Americans. In order to persuade India to sign the NPT, the nuclear powers sponsoring the treaty pledged immediate assistance to any non-nuclear state which was a "victim of an act or object of a threat of aggression in which nuclear weapons were used." It was obvious to everyone that China was the potential nuclear aggressor against whom assistance was promised. But this pledge failed to convince India. France, too, refused to sign the NPT, but this was merely a gesture of Gaullist independence, for the French government made it clear that in practice it would adhere to the treaty provisions.

The Chinese interpretation was that the NPT foreshadowed an American-Soviet military alliance directed against China. This was not entirely fanciful. Soon after the conclusion of the NPT debate Soviet diplomats began to talk openly of the "yellow peril." Mao's China was presented as a deadly menace to the whole civilized world. A seemingly off-hand remark in the beginning of 1969 by Yakov Malik, the Soviet ambassador, was revealing. A veteran Soviet diplomat of the Stalinist school, Malik carefully stuck to the current liturgy in official discussions, but sometimes dropped interesting hints on social occasions when no other Soviet official was present. It was on such an occasion that he suddenly asked me whether I had watched a "politically very significant film" on television the night before. He referred to an old historical film about the siege of Peking at the turn of the century, when an international military force including both American and Russian troops had put down the Boxer rebellion in China. Indeed, Henry Kissinger has written, there can hardly be any doubt that around that time the Soviet leaders contemplated the possibility of a "surgical strike" to eliminate China's nuclear arms production facilities.[21]

In the end, the great majority of UN members resigned themselves to the inequality of power reflected in the NPT and voted for endorsement. Only four countries — the "Peking lobby" — voted against it. But a significant number — twenty one — abstained. Most of these still refuse to sign or ratify the treaty. Among them are at least half of dozen countries which are considered capable of producing nuclear weapons: Argentina, Brazil, India, Israel, Pakistan and South Africa. Of these, India has already conducted a nuclear explosion test for "peaceful purposes." If any one of these countries were to cross the threshold into the nuclear club, the non-proliferation regime would be in danger of coming apart. As the superpowers now begin to reduce their own nuclear arsenals, they will be more anxious than ever to reinforce the NPT. In 1995 a conference is to be convened to determine its future. It will be a crucial test of the ability of the international community to build a peaceful international order.

The Nixon-Brezhnev Pact

Back in 1967, the NPT, despite its fragility, was judged by the superpowers to provide enough protection against a spread of nuclear weapons to justify the launching of Strategic Arms Limitation Talks (SALT). The SALT treaty set ceilings on the number of strategic weapons each side was permitted to have, but as arms technology was left out of control, the effect was to accelerate the nuclear arms race, not to stop it.

The real significance of SALT I, which was signed during President Richard Nixon's visit to Moscow in May 1972, was symbolic. It was a Nixon-Brezhnev non-aggression pact with profound implications for rest of the world. On the way to the Moscow summit each side had demonstrated its devotion to Realpolitik as its supreme guide. Neither side had allowed ideological considerations to stand in the way. The occupation of Czechoslovakia by Warsaw Pact troops in the fall of 1968 had been treated by the West, in the words of a French politician, as "a traffic accident on the road to détente." The Soviet leaders in turn did not let the bombing of the Haiphong harbor in North Vietnam by the US Air Force spoil the friendly atmosphere of the Moscow summit.

The essence of the Nixon-Brezhnev pact was contained in the statement that in the nuclear age the two superpowers must conduct themselves with restraint so as to avoid confrontation. The implications for the UN were obvious, though it is highly unlikely that either party at the Moscow summit had given the world organization any thought. In order to avoid confrontations the two superpowers had to act together to contain regional conflicts before they could get out of hand. For this purpose they would need the services of the UN.

As a result, the long-drawn-out dispute about the authority of the Secretary-General lost its meaning. Even before the Moscow summit, in December 1971, the United States and the Soviet Union had been able to agree on Kurt Waldheim, the Austrian diplomat, as successor to U Thant: he was not a man known for independent action. After the summit, in September in 1972, Henry Kissinger declared in his first speech as Secretary of State that the United States was prepared to consider how the Security Council could play a more central role in the conduct of peacekeeping operations. The aftermath of the Yom Kippur war in the Middle East in October 1973 provided the first test of this change in United States policy. On October 25 the Security Council decided to set up a UN emergency force "under its authority." The practical implications of this phrase became quickly apparent. Each step taken by the Secretary-General to carry out the Council's decision was submitted to the Council itself for approval. The appointment of the force commander was explicitly endorsed, and so was the composition of the force. For the first time in history a member of the Warsaw Pact, Poland, was included in peacekeeping operations. Detailed reports were distributed to the members of the Council on a daily basis. Its authority of the Council was indeed supreme. The Soviets were satisfied: Hammarskjöld's ghost had finally been exorcised. Accordingly Moscow had no objection to paying its share of the operation. At last, it seemed, the UN would be able, in Kissinger's words, "to act swiftly, confidently and effectively in future crises."[22]

In fact, however, fifteen years passed before the UN was able to again act effectively to keep the peace. Soon after the Yom Kippur war American-Soviet collaboration in the UN began to unravel. This was caused by a combination of factors: the post-Vietnam, post-Nixon malaise in the United States; the growth of Soviet military power, particularly at sea; the oil shock and Third World militancy; in short, the Soviets perceived a change in the world balance of power which gave them an edge that made cooperation less necessary. And in the UN, a more specific factor put an end to the American-Soviet partnership that had evolved since the mid-1960s — the entry of the People's Republic of China.

After Henry Kissinger's secret visit to Peking in July 1971, during which agreement was reached for President Nixon to visit China some months later, the United States could no longer prevent the General Assembly from deciding, in October 1971, that the seat of China in the UN belonged to the representatives of the People's Republic. Once Mao's men were in, Soviet tactics in the UN had to change. In Soviet eyes, Communist China was not only a threat to Soviet security in the traditional sense: it was also a rival for leadership in the revolutionary process in the Third World. The Soviets feared that continued collaboration with imperialist America would permit the

Chinese to outflank them from the left in order to gain ascendancy in Asia, Africa and Latin America. Thus Chinese-Soviet rivalry opened the floodgates to the great wave of Third World radicalism which almost drove the United States out of the UN altogether.

The return to confrontation in the UN did not mean an end to détente in Europe. In August 1975, at the moment Daniel Patrick Moynihan as United States ambassador to the UN saw himself mounting a last-ditch defense of Western civilization against the global onslaught of the combined forces of totalitarian socialism, the heads of state or government of the 35 nations of Europe and North America celebrated in Helsinki the high feast of détente by signing the Final Act of the Conference on Security and Cooperation in Europe (CSCE). For the Soviet leaders the ceremony signified fulfillment of their longstanding goal, of legitimizing the territorial and political changes brought about by the second world war. Having secured West Germany's acceptance of the NPT, Moscow now achieved the other goals of its European policy: recognition by the West of the existence of two sovereign German states and of the inviolability of the frontiers agreed upon at the end of the second world war.

The West had neither the will nor the means to challenge Soviet hegemony over the countries the Red Army had occupied in 1945. It had no desire to question the division of Germany into two states. It accepted the status quo as the basis for peace and security in Europe. But it did succeed in Helsinki to write into the Final Act provisions to ensure a freer flow of persons, information and ideas across the dividing line.

The idea of peaceful change was at first dismissed by most observers as either a naive illusion or cynical lipservice. As American-Soviet tensions sharpened, it remained dormant. But what had not been foreseen by Moscow — or by Washington for that matter — was that the Helsinki conference, originally intended to be a conclusion, turned out to be a beginning. The Final Act was not the last word. It gave birth to what in modern diplomatic jargon is called a "process": a string of follow-up conferences dealing with all major issues of common interest to the European countries. Within the Soviet bloc it kept alive hope of change and provided a legal basis for the struggle for human rights.

The contrast between the harmony at the Helsinki conference and the bitter rethoric at the UN revealed that, while an armistice had been reached between East and West in Europe, the cold war was being fought with ever greater intensity in the Third World. And the UN was at its center.

A Dangerous Place?

The UN as the theater of international politics plays to a global audience, but as a function of geography affects Americans, especially New Yorkers, more directly than others. For the great majority of mankind, the UN is a remote institution; for Americans it is a visible presence, an extension of their own political system. Many of the United States representatives to the UN — Henry Cabot Lodge, Adlai Stevenson, Arthur Goldberg, George Bush, Patrick Moynihan, Andrew Young, Jeane Kirkpatrick — have used it as a platform from which to address the American public and advance their own political careers.

The founding fathers of the UN decided to establish the headquarters of the world organization in New York to make sure that the UN would not suffer the fate of the League of Nations. The United States must not once again abandon its creation: the umbilical cord was left uncut.

All went well as long as the right side kept winning. Americans rejoiced when the General Assembly voted to partition Palestine and pave the way to the creation of the state of Israel. They cheered their own men in the great cold war debates and indignantly booed every Soviet veto. They applauded Adlai Stevenson when he confronted the Soviet representative in the Security Council with evidence of the missiles in Cuba. Americans enjoyed watching Nikita Khrushchev, the peasant leader of the Soviet Union, bang his desk with his shoe in frustration over the supercilious tone in which Prime Minister Harold Macmillan of Britain was addressing the General Assembly. They were fascinated by such exotic performances as that of Ali Bhutto of Pakistan who, in the Security Council debate on the Indo-Pakistan war in 1971, spoke for eight hours, pausing only once for a brief fainting spell.

But Americans turned off in revulsion when, in the early 1970s, the sacred drama was twisted into Grand Guignol, a horror show with an anti-American and anti-Israel plot with Yasser Arafat and Idi Amin in star roles. Its climax was reached in 1975, when the General Assembly by 72 votes against 35, with 32 abstentions, adopted a resolution equating Zionism with racism.

For the Arabs the victory in the Assembly vote was vicarious revenge for the defeat on the battlefield. Verbal aggression, according to an Arab sociologist, "enables the Arab to feel that he has overcome his powerlessness." But voting power in the General Assembly is not real power. Assembly resolutions are mere recommendations, not binding decisions. Many resolutions have been ignored and forgotten. As Abba Eban, the former foreign minister of Israel, used to say, if the right group of delegations proposes a resolution asserting that the earth is flat, it would be carried by a large majority. Its supporters could vote for it in the confident knowledge that it would not make the earth flat.

Yet the resolution on Zionism and racism was not ignored and has not been forgotten. It became a turning point in American perceptions of the UN. And though the United States no longer dominates the Organization politically and financially as it used to, American perceptions still tend to determine what is called world opinion. Just as ratings conferred by American financial analysts set the terms on which countries are able to borrow money in the international market, so do the views of American political commentators radiate throughout the international community and influence what people everywhere think of the UN: Is it a success or a failure? In 1975, the judgment was unequivocal. The UN was not only a failure, but much worse: it had become "a dangerous place."

The phrase was used by Daniel Patrick Moynihan as the title of his book recording his eight months, in 1975–76, as US permanent representative to the UN. More than any other individual Moynihan made sure that the resolution on Zionism would not be ignored or forgotten. He rejected the view that the Arabs were merely acting out their frustrations, the way an angry crowd burns in effigy an enemy too powerful to attack in person. The verbal assault against Israel in the UN was in his view something far more sinister. It was part of a world wide campaign, financed by oil money and backed by the Soviet Union, to isolate Israel diplomatically and weaken its economy by a commercial boycott, in preparation for the next round in the armed struggle. The UN resolutions were ammunition used in psychological warfare. By equating her with South Africa as a racist state the Arabs hoped to make Israel an outlaw in the eyes of the international community and condition world opinion to acquiesce in the physical destruction of the Jewish state.

Israel, a vulnerable outpost, was the immediate target, but the ultimate aim of what was believed to be a concerted action of the combined forces of the Soviet Union and the radical nations of the Third World was to weaken the will of the United States and undermine its credibility as defender of the basic values of the Western democracies. In this sense the UN General Assembly had become an important battleground in the great contest between the two world systems, liberal democracy versus totalitarian socialism. It was a contest in which the West at the time felt itself to be on the defensive; as Allen Dulles once put it, like an aging champion grown soft and flabby with good living facing a lean and tough challenger. With the United States humiliated in Vietnam and tarnished by Watergate, Western opinion-makers tended to judge the two systems by a double standard: liberal democracy by its actual performance, socialism by its promise of a better future.

The self-confidence of the market economies had been shattered by the oil crisis in 1973. Western societies were racked with self-doubt, with guilt about the past and pessimism about the future. The Soviet Union, in contrast, seemed to stand for stability and order, confident in its ability to sustain a steady improvement in living standards under conditions of social equality and security.

To the leaders of many countries in the Third World, the Soviet Union offered a superior model of economic progress under social control. Moscow also offered a virtually inexhaustible supply of arms. With Soviet support, the radical elements in the Third World believed they could use the power of oil to bring the industrial countries of the West to their knees. The New International Economic Order — a redistribution of the world's wealth in favour of the peoples of the Third World — appeared at last to take shape.

Behind the verbal attacks against Western positions in the UN the ominous growth of Soviet military power loomed ever larger. After President Richard Nixon's visit to Moscow in 1972, Soviet Foreign Minister Andrei Gromyko was able to make the confident statement that no longer could any important international issue be settled without the participation of the Soviet Union. The Soviet leaders seemed to believe the correlation of forces in the world had shifted decisively in their favour — an assessment widely accepted among Western analysts. Adam Ulam, for instance, wrote in 1976 that "the Soviet Union under Brezhnev had achieved the leading, if not yet the dominant position in world politics." This was the conventional wisdom.

In the UN there was no doubt that the balance of voting power had changed decisively. The majority that could once be rallied almost automatically behind an American position had disappeared. By the beginning of the 1970s the Afro-Asian group had become the dominant bloc, and within it the 22 Arab states exercised a powerful influence. Almost anything they put forward was assured of a two-thirds majority. The states of the Third World, backed by the Soviet Union and its allies, used their voting power in the General Assembly to confer legitimacy to their own ideas and aspirations.

Ironically, the notion that resolutions adopted by the General Assembly represented "world opinion" or the voice of the "conscience of mankind" had originally been promoted by the United States, but similar claims made by the new majority were dismissed by Americans as blasphemy: as a perversion of the original purpose of the UN, an institution created by the United States and intended by its founders, in the words of President Ronald Reagan, to "stand for certain values" — that is, Western values. It became fashionable to belittle the significance of General Assembly resolutions on the ground that voting power had no relation to real power: The Maldive Islands had an equal voice with the United States. (But the vote of the Maldive Islands was not counted out by the United States when the Assembly voted to condemn the Soviet invasion of Afghanistan.)

In December 1974, John A. Scali, Moynihan's predecessor as permanent representative, warned the General Assembly that attempts to browbeat the US and other Western countries by "the tyranny of the majority" would make them turn away from the UN, which would reduce its importance. Moynihan went a step further by dramatizing his role as defender of Western civilization against the barbarians at the gates. He believed in striking back at those who criticized the United States and the West by telling the truth about the oppression and injustices in their own countries.

President Jimmy Carter took a different tack. He sent Andrew Young to the UN, the first black to be named to the job, to put the United States on "the right side of the moral issues of the world" and to persuade the Third World that the United States was determined to make greater use of the UN. But President Reagan put an end to that. He brought to the White House a militantly unilateralist philosophy. By cutting down the US contribution to the UN, in terms of political interest as well as money, the Reagan administration shunted the Organization to the sidelines in international politics. The whole UN system was declared inefficient and wasteful, a nest of Soviet spies. The withdrawal of the United States, followed by Britain and Singapore, from UNESCO seemed to hint at the possibility of even more drastic action to come. "A world without a UN" was discussed as a serious prospect.[23] Public opinion polls showed that an increasing number of Americans had lost confidence in the world body.

Addressing the General Assembly in September 1983, President Reagan spoke to the delegates in the injured tone of a father who has been let down by his favorite son. He reminded them of the original vision of the Assembly as a "great global town meeting" in which member states voted on the merits of issues, free from bloc pressures, and urged them to "regain the dream the UN once dreamt."

The dream was the dream of the essential unity of mankind: All men were the same under the skin, all the peoples of the world want basically the same things from life.

Eventually, according to this vision, the world would become a global melting-pot. Smaller states were expected to merge into larger associations, a development considered not only inevitable but also desirable. Nationalism, the cause of two world wars, would be eradicated. Peace and progress could only be secured through an international organization which, in the words of President Harry Truman, would "establish a world-wide rule of reason." The United States had failed to grasp the chance offered by the League of Nations to establish such an order; it must not fail a second time. In the "American century" proclaimed by Henry Luce in Life magazine, the United States had to take the lead to create a world based on American values.

But Stalin too had his dream. In the Marxist-Leninist view, the class struggle transcended national differences: socialism was the force that inevitably would unite the world. By saying "no" to the Marshall plan, Stalin refused to enter the American world system. The world was divided into two opposing camps, and the contest between the two ideologies became the dominant theme in international politics.

Ancient Feuds

The aspirations of the founding fathers of the UN had a strong hold over American opinion. The American astronaut, who in 1979 was the first man to view the Earth from the moon, exclaimed he could see no frontiers on the surface of our globe: a statement clearly meant to be more than an observation of a physical fact. Yet there are today more frontiers dividing the surface of Earth than ever before. The dream of One World was based on assumptions that proved to be profoundly mistaken. Instead of irresistible progress toward greater political unity, the decades after the second world war have been a time of continued fragmentation of political authority. The membership of the UN has tripled in forty years. Nationalism has ceased to be a dirty word. No longer an aggressive or expansionist doctrine, it has become the last defense of peoples against the anonymous forces of integration that threaten their identity. Peoples and nations not only demand to be recognized as equal with others; they also insist on their right to be different. Contrary to beliefs widely held at the end of the second world war, ideologies have failed to engage the loyalty of peoples: national interest has proved to be a stronger force.

American opinion has been slow to grasp that the ideological world view fostered by the cold war was a misleading description of reality. Washington continued to believe in the existence of a China-Soviet bloc long after the differences between the national interests of the Soviet Union and China had caused an irrevocable rift between them. American policymakers kept adding up the divisions of the

Warsaw Pact on the misguided assumption that Poles and Hungarians would march against the West on Moscow's orders or that Germans would start killing other Germans for the sake of an ideology most of them had never believed in. American reactions to nationalism continued to be ambiguous or hypocritical. A noble stand against tyranny in one part of the world becomes an atavistic impulse in another. The Baltic nations were first applauded for their struggle to regain independence, then advised by Western governments not to make trouble for Gorbachev. The Palestinians are glorified by the media, but the Basques are condemned as terrorists, Welsh and Scottish nationalism is dismissed as quixotic, the Kurds are simply forgotten.

Throughout the world, ancient feuds and rivalries, rather than ideological differences, are the source of violence — between Armenians and Azerbaidzhanis, Serbs and Croats, Arabs and Persians, Jews and Palestinians, Sikhs and Hindus, Tamils and Sinhalese, Tutsis and Huttus in Burundi, Protestants and Catholics in Northern Ireland, Turks and Greeks in Cyprus.

In a world torn by strife and tension, the UN could hardly become an idealized version of a town meeting where members consider issues on their merits: Is there such an assembly anywhere in the world? The dream remains a dream. But surely the UN is no longer the nightmare many Americans had come to believe it to be.

By the end of the 1980s, the analysis Moynihan and other American critics had put forward had been overtaken by events. The socialist promise of a better future has lost its credibility. The Soviet system is in deep crisis. Communism no longer attracts young people. In Europe, once powerful communist parties have been reduced to playing a marginal role in the political life of their countries. Throughout the world, from Algeria to Zambia, attempts are being made to revive stagnant socialist economies based on the Soviet model by injections of private enterprise.

Oil, once again, has been a catalyst. The oil boom of the 1970s tripled the export earnings of the Soviet Union and created a lucrative market for Soviet arms in the oil-producing countries of the Third World. The rise in the gold price further strengthened the Soviet position. Now Soviet economists say this was a great misfortune for their country. It created a false sense of wealth and power. It enabled the Brezhnev regime to shelve the economic reforms that had been planned in the 1960s. The fall in the oil price in the 1980s exposed the true state of the Soviet economy. The urgent need for reform finally became inescapable.

In the Third World, too, the change in the structure of the world economy had a sobering effect. A "creeping pragmatism" is eroding ideological positions built up during the 1960s and the 1970s. The political leaders of the developing countries are now less interested in changing the world by political action and more absorbed in the task of improving the economic conditions of their own people. Ideologues like Qaddafi of Libya or Kim Il Sung of North Korea stand out as bizarre exceptions. The growing economic disparities between the countries of Asia, Africa and Latin America have reduced the political cohesion of the Third World to empty rhetoric.

Israel is no longer the vulnerable outpost she seemed to be in the 1970s. The campaign to isolate her has failed. It was of course effectively broken by President Anwar Sadat as early as in 1977, but it took another ten years before Egypt was readmitted into the Arab fold, and the Soviet Union and its allies reestablished ties with the Jewish state. Israel continues to face formidable problems, but her existence is not now threatened by an armed attack by the combined forces of the Arab states backed by Soviet power.

The wind of change blowing across the world could be felt in the UN well before the demand for peacekeeping services stirred up renewed public interest in the Organization. Jolted by the US withdrawal from UNESCO, the General Assembly in 1986 finally initiated a financial and administrative cleanup. The wave of Third World radicalism subsided. From 1988 on, sessions of the General Assembly have been markedly consensus-minded. Most important of all, the Soviet Union under Gorbachev has declared a strong interest in making the UN a central organ of international cooperation across the ideological divisions. The new Soviet initiatives are addressed primarily to the United States. Indeed, it would not be too far fetched to see in them an attempt to revive something of the original impulse that led to the creation of the world organization.

What this means for the UN is that the line is drawn more clearly than ever between, on the one hand, the affairs of rich and powerful nations and, on the other, the rest of the world. European security, European disarmament, European economic, environmental and human rights issues will be dealt with within the framework of the CSCE process. They will not be brought to the UN. The UN is where the developed world meets the developing world. Will it be possible in the 1990s for the developed world to find a more united and thus more constructive approach to the problems of the developing world? The answer to this question depends to a great extent on how one reads the pronouncements that have been recently emanating from Moscow.

The Gorbachev Message

The sudden outpouring from Moscow of support for the UN raised great hope among westerners who continued to believe in the importance of the world organization and distressed by its decline. "To hear Moscow talk, the United Nations has a future,"[24] according to one headline. But among policymakers in Washington and other Western capitals hope was liberally laced with suspicion: What are the Russians up to now?

To suspect Soviet motives is of course a reflex action on the part of every Western diplomat. But differences in political culture and tradition also stand in the way of mutual understanding. Soviet documents filled with elaborate and excessive verbiage are screened by American analysts looking for a catch. Most likely there is none: this is just part of the Soviet trimming in which they wrap the message.

The Kremlin and the White House are opposite poles in their modes of operation. American presidents tend to act first, then instruct one of the clever academics on their staff to write it up into a foreign policy doctrine. The rulers of Russia will not take a single step before emitting a dense smokescreen of philosophical declarations.

When Czar Alexander I in 1815 read out his first draft of the Holy Alliance to the Duke of Wellington and British Foreign Secretary Lord Castleraigh, the two Englishmen were bewildered. Castleraigh reported to London that "it was not without difficulty that we went through the interview with becoming gravity." The Czar's text was a "piece of sublime mysticism and nonsense." Count Metternich, the Austrian Chancellor, called it a "loud sounding nothing."[25] Yet the political concept underlying the flowery phrases was tough enough to hold Europe in an iron grip for decades.

At the close of the century, in August 1898, a Russian initiative once again astonished and bewildered the world. This was the call issued by Czar Nicholas II to the nations to join in a conference for the limitation of armaments. "The intellectual and physical strength of nations," he declared, "have been unproductively consumed in building terrible engines of destruction." Weapons that are today the last word in science, tomorrow will be obsolete and need to be replaced. The arms race had become a crushing burden on all nations and, if prolonged, would inevitably lead to the very catastrophe it was designed to avert.

The Czar's appeal struck a chord in the Western world where the peace movement had gained great strength. The belief that war had become impossible "except at the price of suicide" had been persuasively propagated by distinguished writers. But there was also a great deal of suspicion of Russia's motives. Kipling wrote his poem "The Bear that Walks like a Man" to warn the British people against trusting the peaceful intentions of the Czar. Experts pointed out that Russia was behind in the arms race and could not afford to spend more on weapons. But in spite of their misgivings the governments of all major powers felt they could not flout public opinion by rejecting the Czar's proposal. The first peace conference was held in the Hague in 1899, where it was agreed to ban projectiles from balloons, asphyxiating gases and expanding bullets. A second Hague conference convened in 1907 which resulted in subsequent conventions refining the rules of warfare. A third peace conference was scheduled for 1915.[26]

The Russian tradition of advancing idealistic proposals for collective security was revived by Mikhail Gorbachev in his landmark speech at the UN General Assembly meeting on December 7, 1988. "World politics should be guided by the primacy of universal human values," he declared, thus discarding the traditional Soviet thesis that the struggle between socialism and capitalism is at the core of international relations and guides the course of Soviet foreign policy. The earlier insistence that peaceful coexistence was a way of carrying on the class struggle gave way to the notion that the common problems of mankind take precedence over the class struggle. "The world economy is becoming a single organism," Gorbachev stated. "No state, whatever its social system or economic status, can normally develop outside it." In a "mutually interrelated and integrated world" it was no longer possible to preserve "a closed society." Neither security nor economic development could be achieved "at the expense of other nations or at the expense of nature." Relations among states must therefore be "deideologized."

Gorbachev was saying that the Soviet Union had abandoned its revolutionary mission and wanted to join the world as a state among other states, prepared to accept the rules of the game and willing to share the burden of coping with the common problems of the international community.

This time, the words were confirmed by deeds. The withdrawal of Soviet troops from Afghanistan proved that Gorbachev meant what he said. It was a sharp break with the past.

Traditionally, Russia has sought security and power by territorial expansion and subjugation of neighboring nations. At the time of the Crimean war, a Russian statesman said that "Russia can feel completely secure only when Russian soldiers stand on both sides of her border." This concept of security has coincided with its quest for empire building. Its spirit was expressed in the famous remark by Czar Nicholas I: "Where the Russian flag has once been hoisted it must never be lowered." Stalin told Tito in April 1945: "Whoever occupies a territory also imposes on it its social system. Everyone imposes his own system as far as his army can reach."[27]

Khrushchev took a few tentative steps in a different direction when, in 1955, he withdrew the Soviet troops from Austria in return for a pledge of Austrian neutrality and abandoned the Soviet military bases in Finland and China. But his successor reverted to traditional Russian policy. Under Brezhnev, the Soviet Union responded to every problem with military means. The ideological challenge of the Prague Spring in 1968 was met with Soviet tanks. A surgical nuclear strike was contemplated against Maoism. The United States was goaded into rearming by the vast expansion of Soviet military influence into Asia and Africa. Japan was alienated by the stationing of Soviet troops on the disputed islands off Hokkaido. Western Europe was frightened by the deployment of the SS20 missiles. Finally, the invasion of Afghanistan turned most of the Islamic world against Moscow. Each of these actions confirmed the primacy of military over political considerations in Soviet decisionmaking. In each case Brezhnev seems to have listened to His Marshals' Voice. Fittingly, before his death, Brezhnev himself was elevated to the honorary rank of Soviet marshal: a gesture symbolizing his complete identification with the militarization of Soviet foreign policy.

The results were disastrous. At the end of the Brezhnev era Soviet relations with all major powers were virtually frozen. The atavistic search for territorial security led to a dead end. The "zone of security" created in Eastern and Central Europe had become a zone of vulnerability. Afghanistan, in the words of Gorbachev himself, was a bleeding wound. The gigantic military machine built up during the Brehznev era to enable the Soviet Union to keep up with the United States as a global superpower had drained the Soviet system of vitality.

The condition of the Soviet Union came to resemble what a mid-nineteenth century Russian writer described as a society that had, "imprisoned within it, fresh forces seething and bursting to break out, but crushed by heavy repression and unable to escape; they produce gloom and bitter depression, apathy." Brezhnev's extreme conservatism stopped the clock for twenty years, preventing the generational cycle from taking its natural course.

The generational cycle is an engine of political change in every society. As de Toqueville wrote, "each generation is a new people." In a country like Russia, which for centuries has lived under autocratic rule and an all-embracing orthodoxy, it is virtually the only opportunity for fundamental reform. Thus Gorbachev came to power, not by defeating the previous incumbent, but by waiting patiently for his death. But once in office, Gorbachev wasted no time in denouncing his predecessors and demanding a sweeping revision — a perestroika — of Soviet policies both at home and abroad. What followed is by now a familiar story and need not be repeated here.

In Gorbachev's grand strategy the UN has an important role to play. The Soviet government is paying more attention to the UN than any other major power and appears to be prepared to invest a considerable effort into revitalizing the Organization. This makes sense in the context of a general policy of retreat from positions no longer tenable. An ascendant power believes it can go it alone; a power in decline discovers the advantages of multilateralism. Burden-sharing implies influence-sharing. Soviet policy in the Persian Gulf crisis is a case in point. By insisting that decisions on collective action against Iraq must be made in the Security Council and by advocating a more active role for the Military Staff Committee, the Soviet government has made sure that it will retain at least some degree of influence over developments in the Middle East.

But clearly Soviet interest in the UN goes beyond such tactical considerations. It is an essential part of the general strategy of modernization. According to Gorbachev's "new thinking," Soviet foreign policy must be made to serve the need of domestic reform. The paramount need of any country engaged in a task of internal reconstruction is peace. Externally, in Gorbachev's words, this means "stable and predictable relations" with other countries. The Soviet Union must be able to reduce its oppressive military burden and obtain as much help as possible from the West in the form of increased trade, credits, investments and know-how. The goal is to integrate the Soviet Union into the developed world system: the way is through the UN, and other international organizations such as the International Monetary Fund, the World Bank and GATT.

Many of the foreign policy initiatives of the Soviet Union are designed to advance the course of reform within the country itself. As John F. Kennedy noted, "All that happens . . . at home has a direct and intimate bearing what we can and must do abroad. All that happens to us abroad has a direct and intimate bearing on what we can and must do at home . . ." Thus, the international commitments the Soviet government has made with regard to human rights are not only part of a campaign to appease Western opinion, but also intended for use at home in support of a reform of the legal system. The interaction between foreign policy and domestic change is also evident in Soviet efforts to deal with environmental problems, drugs, aids and terrorism. Before Gorbachev, the official line was that the socialist system, by definition, was immune to such problems. Now Soviet authorities not only admit they exist in their country, but are also anxious to benefit from international cooperation in dealing with them.

This time East-West détente has not been limited to Europe. The reappraisal of Soviet interests carried out by Gorbachev had extended to the Third World as well.

The expansion of Soviet influence in Asia, Africa and Latin America had been motivated by old-fashioned imperialism rather than by ideological zeal. The romantic notion entertained by Khrushchev that the national liberation movements in the former colonies would pave the way to a victory of world revolution had been discarded long ago. Under Brehznev, Soviet influence in the Third World was backed up by arms and soldiers rather than by Marxist missionaries. The invasion of Afghanistan was justified by Soviet diplomats as a civilizing mission. Countries like Vietnam, Syria, Libya, South Yemen, Ethiopia, Angola and Mozambique — each embroiled in armed conflict — became dependent on arms and military advisers either from the Soviet Union itself or one of its allies. Cuba remained Moscow's outpost in the Latin American region, from where Soviet influence could be extended to Central America and beyond. At the beginning of the 1970s the Soviet leaders could claim that their country had graduated from a regional power to the rank of a superpower with global reach.

But at what cost? Through its various clients the Soviet Union became involved, directly or indirectly, in perpetual warfare around the globe. The extension of political influence brought no economic benefit; on the contrary, every one of the allies had to be subsidized. And the political costs were incalculable. In the United States, in particular, the expansion of Soviet power in the Third World was perceived as a bid for world domination and provided a strong impulse to the Reagan rearmament program.

Under Gorbachev, Moscow started cutting its losses. "The bell of every regional conflict tolls for all of us," Gorbachev declared in his UN speech. Moscow now recognized that the Third World was a source of instability and risk — a minefield of potentially explosive crises that might damage efforts to improve Soviet relations with the West.

The change in Soviet policy toward the Third World had a direct effect on the UN. One of the first signals of a shift in Soviet policy was Moscow's willingness in 1987 to help remove the African Director-General of UNESCO, Amabu Mahdar M'bow, who had become in American eyes a symbol of everything rotten in the UN system. In the UN itself, the Soviet delegation began to support American demands for administrative and financial reform. It discouraged the Third World countries from seeking futile voting victories which only alienate Western opinion and thus reduce the usefulness of the UN. Indeed, at the 1988 General Assembly session the Soviets declared themselves in favor of adopting important resolutions by consensus. The effect on the more radical Third World delegations was sobering. They no longer could depend on the Soviet Union and its allies to join in propaganda campaigns against the United States.

"We were wrong not to support peacekeeping, we were wrong to oppose an independent role for the Secretary-General," admitted Deputy Foreign Minister Vladimir Petrovsky, one of the architects of the new Soviet policy in the UN, in July 1988: a sensational statement to anyone like myself who had been involved in the bitter doctrinal disputes on these issues in the 1960s.[28] The Soviet government now not only accepts the legitimacy of UN peacekeeping activities, it has become one of the most enthusiastic advocates of a wider and more active UN role, under the leadership of the Secretary-General, in conflict prevention. This dramatic shift in the Soviet position has opened up, for the first time in 45 years, a real possibility of making effective use of UN services in the interest of international peace and stability.

But will it last? Internal developments in the Soviet Union cast grave doubt on Gorbachev's ability to hold on to the course of reform. His many Western admirers have been disappointed to discover that his priorities are not what they had imagined. From the outset his goal has been to stop the decline of the Soviet Union as a great power. Perestroika was a means to that end. Democratization was meant to replace the old guard with Gorbachev's men; glasnost to reveal the mistakes and failures of the Brezhnev regime. But when democratization threatened to lead to a breakup of the Soviet Union and glasnost turned into criticism of current policies, Gorbachev reverted to autocratic rule, relying on the forces of the old order — the military, the KGB, the Communist party bureaucracy — to restore discipline and keep the empire from falling apart. He insists that reforms will be continued, but in the Russian Tradition — from above.

The democratic movement demonstrates its strength in Moscow and Leningrad, but the vast majority of the population lives in a state of ignorance and apathy unaffected by all the talk of democracy or a market economy. In view of the archaic structure of Soviet industry, the bitter feuds between ethnic groups condemned to live intermingled with each other and the horrifying environmental damage caused by decades of pollution, it would be wildly optimistic to expect either economic progress or internal political stability in the near future.

Amidst all his troubles, Gorbachev keeps assuring the outside world that his foreign policy will remain on course. Since it is a policy dictated by economic necessity, there is no reason to doubt his sincerity. His ability to carry out his intentions is another matter. The outcome of the struggle convulsing the Soviet Union is uncertain. Gorbachev's "new thinking" is a heroic attempt to break down powerful elements in the Russian Tradition. It is at the heart of the age-old conflict between the modernizers who want to open the door to the influence of European enlightenment and rationalism and the latter-day followers of the slavophiles who, like Solzhenitzyn, despise the decadence of the West and are prepared to forego the blessings of its superior technology in favor of what they consider higher spiritual values. The Soviet Union — Russia — may yet retreat into sullen isolation.

For the UN, this would mean a less cooperative, perhaps even obstructionist Soviet Union. But it would not mean a return to thee paralysis of the cold war. An isolationist Soviet Union would stand alone, without allies, unable to mobilize support among the Third World countries. If it were to use its veto to prevent action by the Security Council, it would cause the United States and its allies to bypass the UN, thus depriving itself of any influence on their decisions.

The West has chosen to support Gorbachev's policy of keeping the empire intact, rather than face the risk of a collapse of central power that might lead to widespread chaos and leave more than 30,000 nuclear weapons up for grabs. At the November 1990 CSCE summit in Paris, the leaders of the 34 participating states refused to let representatives of the Baltic nations attend the conference as guests: stability was put before the principle of national self-determination. By establishing permanent institutions for the CSCE process, the summit created, in effect, a regional security order for Europe, a White Man's UN, thus formally confirming the exclusion of European issues from the world organization.

The Turning Point

An exploration of what the end of the cold war has meant for the UN can begin with the meeting of the Security Council on 20 July, 1987. This was the day the Council stirred out of the comatose condition it had been in for a decade and began to take notice of what was going on in the world. The savage war between Iran and Iraq was about to enter its eighth year. At last the Council decided to do something to stop it.

Until that date the Security Council, the body charged with "primary responsibility for the maintenance of international peace and security," had made only feeble attempts to deal with the war. It had ignored the mounting tension between Iran and Iraq which in the spring and summer of 1980 had provided ample warning of what was to follow. On September 22, 1980, Iraqi aircraft struck at targets deep inside Iran, and on the next day Iraqi ground forces invaded in strength. On September 28 the Security Council adopted a resolution calling for an immediate end to the use of force and urged both sides to accept any appropriate offer of mediation, but the resolution made no reference to Iraqi aggression nor did it demand a withdrawal of forces to their own frontiers. The Iranian government refused to enter into any discussions while Iraqi forces remained on Iranian soil.

After this rebuff the Council remained silent for almost two years. The mediation effort of the late Olof Palme of Sweden, as special representative of Secretary-General Pérez de Cuellar, petered out for lack of support from the Security Council. In June 1984, the Secretary-General succeeded in getting both parties to agree to a moratorium on attacks against civilian targets, but this arrangement lasted only nine months. The Secretary-General also sent a mission under his own authority to investigate charges of the use of chemical weapons by Iraqi forces and reported to the Council that such weapons had indeed been employed. But not even this aroused the Council: its only reaction was to issue a mild rebuke in the form of a statement by its president.[29]

The Iranians complained that the Security Council was biased in favour of their enemy, and they were quite right. But the charge is irrelevant. The Council is not a tribunal, the 15 men or women sitting around its horseshoe table are no judges. They are diplomats acting on behalf of their governments. A Council decision is a blend of the national interests of its member states distilled by a process of behind-the-scenes consultations. In the case of the Iran-Iraq war, the blend was poison to the Iranians.

The question of which side had committed aggression was not quite as clearcut as it seemed. According to the Charter, "The Security Council shall determine the existence of . . . an act of aggression." A UN committee of lawyers labored for years to define what constitutes aggression and finally in 1974 came up with an agreed text, but in reality the decision is always made on political rather than juridical grounds. In the case of the Iran-Iraq war, it could be claimed that Khomeini's call to Iraq's Shi'ite majority to rise up and establish an Islamic regime was a form of indirect aggression which forced Iraq to act in self-defense. It could even be argued, though no one said so aloud, that the cause of international peace and security would best be served by allowing Iraq to knock out the Khomeini regime whose revolutionary activities were causing trouble throughout the Islamic world.

The Council's vapid reaction to the use of gas by Iraq provided a revealing glimpse of the realities behind the rhetoric heard in the Security Council chamber. Everyone, is of course, against the use of chemical weapons. Indeed, "the fear of poison is written in our genes."[30] But that very fear makes gas an effective weapon of last resort. Many people are convinced that chemical weapons won the war for Iraq. They also were used by Iraq against its own Kurdish civilians: another victim who has no powerful sponsor in the international community. Again Iraq got off with a reprimand. Now all the permanent members of the Security Council loudly proclaim their unreserved support for a ban of chemical weapons. But leaders of Third World countries have taken note of the fact that the Iraqis used gas effectively and got away with it.

The evasive maneuvers of the Security Council were part of the tangled web of American-Soviet rivalries, the conflicting interests of the other states in the region and the shadowy activities of the arms merchants. (In 1980–88, Iraq spent $ 47.3 billion and Iran $ 717.5 billion in arms purchases. Sales to the two countries accounted for 21.5 percent of arms sales by all suppliers to the Third World.)[31] The Soviet Union was tied down in Afghanistan, while American hostility towards the Khomeini regime was tempered by the need to support the Mudjahedin who were fighting the Russians next door. The conservative Arab states in the Gulf region feared the militant fundamentalism propagated by Iran. France had close economic and military ties with Iraq. No one would have mourned the passing of the Khomeini regime, except the Israelis for whom war without end between their two enemies was the best thing that had happened for a long time.

As relations between the United States and the Soviet Union became increasingly strained in the first half of the 1980s, no common ground could be found in the Security Council on the Iran-Iraq war, or on any other important issue. The Secretary-General was left to act on his own on behalf of international peace and security. Without the backing of the major powers he had no chance of success, but it would be a mistake to dismiss his efforts as unimportant. The trust Pérez de Cuellar gained on both sides as a reliable and objective go-between was a valuable asset that paid dividends as soon as the power constellation began to change.

The first hint of a change came in the beginning of 1987. The Secretary-General convened on January 16 a meeting of the representatives of the permanent members of the Security Council (Britain, China, France, the Soviet Union and the United States) and outlined to them his thoughts on how Iran and Iraq might be persuaded to stop the war. The response of both the United States and the Soviet Union was cautiously favorable. It was no longer possible to believe that Iraq might finish off Khomeini. Instead, the war was beginning to spill over into a wider international conflict. Shipping in the Persian Gulf was under attack. The United States had made it clear that it would not tolerate a closing of the Gulf; the Soviet Union on its part watched with apprehension the increase in American military activity in the region.

It took six months of discreet negotiations for the five permanent members to agree on a text of a Security Council resolution to show to the ten non-permanent members. On July 20, the Council finally held an official meeting and unanimously adopted Resolution 598 demanding an immediate cease-fire between Iran and Iraq and a withdrawal of all forces to the internationally recognized boundaries. It requested the Secretary-General to dispatch a team of UN observers to supervise the disengagement and called upon Iran and Iraq to cooperate with the Secretary-General to achieve a comprehensive settlement of all outstanding issues. As a sop to Iran the resolution requested the Secretary-General to explore the question of entrusting an impartial body with the task of enquiring into responsibility for the conflict, and as a carrot to both parties, it authorized the Secretary-General to assign a team of experts to study the need for international assistance for reconstruction.

Two months later, on September 25, the foreign ministers of the Big Five met with the Secretary-General at the UN to state publicly their determination to secure full and rapid implementation of Resolution 598. For the UN which for so many years had been starved of high level attention, this was a spectacular event, like a surprise appearance of Broadway stars at a provincial theater. Even the media took notice: the UN was back at the center of world politics.

"With words we govern men," Disraeli noted, but word issued from New York failed to govern the men fighting along the Persian Gulf. The Secretary-General was rebuffed by Iran. The killing went on. At the UN the mood reverted to despondent resignation. Had the SecretaryGeneral missed his chance? Old hands began to mutter about what Dag Hammarskjöld might have done. Once again, the media observed, the UN had failed.

The image of the UN as an autonomous actor in world politics has become so deeply imbedded in our habits of thought and speech that even those who know better tend to use expressions implying belief in the power of the UN to make nations — nations other than their own — obey its commands. Soon after the adoption of Resolution 598 I had the opportunity to ask Secretary of State George Shultz, the chief architect of the Security Council resolution, whether the United States now might revise its attitude to the UN and give it more support. He replied curtly: "Let the UN first show it can get results." But the lack of results in the Persian Gulf was due to the failure of the major powers, including the United States, to back up the Security Council resolution with enough authority and enough resources. They failed to agree on what seemed a necessary next step: a joint decision to cut off the supply of arms to both warring parties.

Another year of fighting, with thousands killed, maimed and gassed on both sides, was needed to achieve the results Mr. Shultz had asked for. In June 1988, the Iranians, hard pressed on the battlefield and exhausted on the home front, finally agreed to a cease-fire. At this point Security Council Resolution 598 turned out to be useful after all. It had not by itself made the parties stop the war. But once the Iranian leaders, for reasons of their own, decided they had had enough, they were able to grasp the hand extended to them by the Secretary-General, instead of having to humiliate themselves before their enemies. Once again, the UN provided a stage for the "sacred drama" of reconciliation.

Now there was elation at the UN. Secretary-General Javier Pérez de Cuellar was proclaimed an instant candidate for the Nobel Peace Prize. (The award was subsequently given to the UN Peacekeeping Forces collectively.) Officers in blue berets were quickly dispatched to the Iran-Iraq front. Suddenly the peacekeeping business was booming. UN observers were busy in Afghanistan and preparations were begun for servicing prospective customers in Namibia, Central America and Western Sahara. The UN, the media concluded, was a success after all.

Success and failure are dangerously misleading terms which ought to be banished from the UN vocabulary. Their use tends to perpetuate the myth of the UN as a power in its own right, with exclusive jurisdiction over the issues on its agenda. In fact, no dispute or conflict between states is dealt with solely through the UN. Consideration of an issue in the UN is usually but one element in a number of influences brought to bear. In the case of the Iran-Iraq war, the means employed by the United States ranged from secret arms deals with Iran to naval action in the Persian Gulf. The unanimous backing Security Council Resolution 598 received from the major powers obviously impressed the Iranian leaders, but so did probably the accidental shooting down of an Iranian airliner by a US destroyer in the Persian Gulf.

What turned "failure" into "success" for the UN in dealing with the Iran-Iraq war and other regional conflicts in the Third World was the great turn of the tide in world affairs — the shift in the "correlation of forces," as Soviet analysts say — that compelled Soviet leaders to reorder their priorities, staunch the bleeding in Afghanistan and abandon farflung outposts, so as to lighten the military burden and pacify the United States and other important powers. Once the superpowers had changed course from confrontation to summitry, their view of the significance of the various regional conflicts that had gone on for years changed almost overnight. These ceased to be vital tests of will, or important battles in a global struggle for supremacy. Instead they became road blocks on the way to disarmament and peace. This meant that nothing could be allowed to undermine efforts to improve the central relationship between the two super powers. Linkage, whether or not explicitly stated, is a fact of life. And linkage brings the UN into the picture. Any understanding reached between the United States and the Soviet Union on settling or containing a conflict in the Third World must be legitimized by UN resolutions, and UN services are usually needed to carry it out in the field.

In the case of the war in Afghanistan, for instance, Soviet President Gorbachev made the withdrawal of Soviet troops contingent on an agreement being reached in the UN-sponsored peacetalks in Geneva. The Geneva Accords, negotiated under the auspices of the UN Secretary-General and guaranteed by both the United States and the Soviet Union, were signed on April 14, 1988, and a month later the troop withdrawal began. A UN observer mission was sent into the field to monitor the withdrawal which was completed in February 1989. No doubt Gorbachev was determined to get out of Afghanistan in any case, and his direct negotiations with the United States provided him with the cover he needed, but the good offices of the Secretary-General were nonetheless essential for ensuring the smoothness of the complex operation.

The Guns of August

While the cease-fire in the Iran-Iraq war and the withdrawal of Soviet troops from Afghanistan proved the usefulness of the UN as a tool for facilitating the resolution of regional conflicts, both cases also revealed the limited and superficial nature of collective action, as it has been practiced so far, to maintain peace and stability in the world.

The attention span of the Security Council is as short as that of a newspaper; no story stays on the front page for very long. Once the Soviet troops had departed, Afghanistan dropped off the agenda, yet the fighting went on, the devastation continued, and millions of refugees remained in limbo. The Secretary-General has gone on trying to help the warring parties to reach a national consensus, but the major powers have taken little interest.

The lack of any follow-up of the cease-fire between Iran and Iraq had even more disastrous consequences. The Western world believed it need no longer worry about the Ayatollah Khomeini and his Islamic fundamentalist aggressiveness; it ignored the secular aggressiveness of Saddam Hussein. His country was thought to be exhausted by eight years of war, weighed down by a huge debt and handicapped by a depressed oil market. The Security Council simply forgot about its promise to look into the postwar reconstruction needs of the two countries. This was a fatal omission.

According to statistics compiled by the Stockholm International Peace Research Institute (SIPRI), Iraq spent in 1984–89 almost twelve billion dollars on purchases of major weapons, most of it on credit. One of the major creditors was Kuwait. By grabbing Kuwait, Saddam Hussein believed he could not only wipe out a major portion of his debts and gain command over half of the Middle East oil resources, he could also claim to have erased the last remnant of the legacy of British imperialism and emerge as the great leader who would unify the "Arab nation" and drive the Jews out of Palestine. Evidently he did not think the United States would stand in his way. In July 1990, Saddam Hussein told the American ambassador in Baghdad that in his view the United States was a society that could not sustain casualties of ten thousand men in a battle. He was not contradicted; the State Department line was that the United States would not interfere in disputes between Arab states. As for the possibility of an Israeli intervention, Saddam Hussein had already warned three months earlier that he would not hesitate to strike back with chemical weapons that could devastate half of the Jewish state.

As so often before in history, the dictator's threats and warnings were dismissed by the democracies as bluff and bluster, while the dictator underestimated the capacity of the democracies to rise to a challenge. The armed forces of Iraq invaded Kuwait on August 2, 1990, and on that same day the Security Council was convened in New York to deal with the crisis. It determined that a breach of international peace and security had taken place and, "acting under Article 34 and 90 of the Charter of the United Nations", condemned the Iraqi invasion and demanded that Iraq withdraw immediately and unconditionally all its forces to the positions they held on August 1, 1990. Four days later, noting that Iraq had failed to comply with the demand, the Council decided to order comprehensive economic sanctions until the sovereignty, independence, and territorial integrity of Kuwait had been restored.

A series of new decisions followed in quick succession. On August 9, the Council declared that Iraq's annexation of Kuwait had no legal validity; on August 18, it demanded that Iraq permit and facilitate the immediate departure of the nationals of third countries from Kuwait and Iraq; on August 25, it called upon member states deploying maritime forces in the Persian Gulf area to halt all inward and outward maritime shipping in order to inspect and verify their cargoes and destinations so as to ensure compliance with economic sanctions. On September 13, the Council agreed to permit the delivery of food to Iraq for humanitarian purposes, but only through the international Red Cross or other appropriate humanitarian agencies; on September 16, it demanded that Iraq protect the safety of diplomatic and consular personnel and take no action to hinder the foreign missions in the performance of their functions. On September 24, it entrusted its sanctions committee to examine requests for economic assistance from countries that had suffered heavy losses as a result of compliance with sanctions. On September 25, it extended the blockade of Iraq to air traffic; on October 29, it warned Iraq that it will be held responsible for any loss, damage or injury caused by the invasion of Kuwait, and finally, on November 29, it issued its ultimatum. If Iraq did not withdraw by

January 15, 1991, the Council authorized "member states co-operating with the government of Kuwait" — that is, the international coalition led by the United States — "to use all necessary means" to implement its resolutions and "to restore international peace and security in the area" — a wide mandate indeed.

The contrast between the swift and stern action initiated by the Council in August 1990 and the leisurely proceedings in response to the Iraqi attack against Iran ten years earlier is dramatic. In institutional terms, the reason is obvious. In 1980, relations between the United States and the Soviet Union were strained; no common action in the Middle East was imaginable. In 1990, the two superpowers were working closely together as partners in settling regional conflicts. In terms of Realpolitik, the reason was oil. The United States, a society hooked on imported oil, could not afford to let a ruthless Arab dictator gain control of a large part of Middle East oil resources. After the conquest of Kuwait, Saudi Arabia might be next. Beyond oil, the credibility of the United States as an ally and protector of Israel and the moderate Arab states was at stake. Washington would have had to act in any case, even in the event the Soviet Union and China had used their veto to prevent a decision by the Security Council. As it was, the United States was able to line up unprecedented international support by cashing every promissory note ever issued to allies, clients and protectorates, and even former adversaries. The Soviet Union joined to prove its credentials as a member of the civilized world community; China used the opportunity to breach the diplomatic boycott she had been subjected to since the Tiananmen massacre; even Syria signed up on the hallowed principle that the enemy of one's enemy is one's friend.

For the UN, the Iraqi attack on Kuwait was an existential challenge. The phrase "naked aggression," so popular in UN oratory, for once fit perfectly. Saddam Hussein did not bother to cover his action with any of the usual fig-leaves. He did not pretend to be the victim of provocation or to act in self-defense. His armies invaded Kuwait to seize its treasures, destroy its government, and annex the country. If this was not called aggression, nothing ever could.

In the UN, aggression is not taken in vain. It is a code word that opens the door to Chapter VII of the Charter entitled "Action with Respect to Threats to the Peace, Breaches of the Peace, and Acts of

Aggression," a catalogue of measures considered so awe-inspiring that in the forty years from the Korean war to the Iraqi attack against Kuwait, Chapter VII was invoked only once, in 1967, to order economic sanctions to compel the white minority regime in Southern Rhodesia to share power with the black majority.

After the Six Day War in June 1967, the Soviet Union tried to persuade the General Assembly to brand Israel as the aggressor, but its proposal was defeated by more than a two-thirds majority — a historical fact of relevance to current attempts to equate the Israeli occupation of the West Bank and Gaza with the Iraqi occupation of Kuwait. Time and again in the past twenty years, the Arab states have tried to persuade the Security Council to apply sanctions against Israel, but so far without success. A few times the Council has gone so far as to warn Israel that a repetition of the use of force might compel it to consider measures under Chapter VII of the Charter. I remember one typical exchange from 1970, when the Egyptian ambassador commented, "What you really mean is that you warn Israel that next time you will warn her again." This just about summed up the situation.

Having determined that the Iraqi invasion of Kuwait was a breach of international peace, the Security Council had no choice but to step on to the escalator of measures prescribed in Chapter VII of the Charter. Thus, according to Article 41, the Council may order measures not involving the use of armed force, such as complete or partial interruption of economic relations and of rail, sea, air, postal, telegraphic, radio, and other means of communication. In the event such sanctions prove inadequate, the Council may decide, according to Article 42, "to take such action by air, sea, or landforces as may be necessary," including "demonstrations, blockade, and other operations by air, sea, or landforces of members of the UN." In plain language, the Council may decide to make war against the aggressor.

What makes Chapter VII different from all other chapters of the Charter is not only the kind of action it prescribes but also the legal quality of resolutions based on it: they are not merely recommendations like all other UN resolutions, but decisions binding upon member states. By invoking Chapter VII the Council thus transforms itself into a supranational directorate with a global authority. The only limitation placed on its war-making power is the right of veto reserved for its five permanent members. All other member states, by joining the UN, have signed away their sovereignty on the issue of war and peace. Not only have they agreed, under Article 27, "to accept and carry out the decisions of the Security Council" they have also undertaken, under Article 43, "to make available to the Security Council . . . armed forces, assistance, and facilities, including rights of passage, necessary for the purpose of maintaining international peace and security" — a commitment most people had forgotten about.

Chapter VII was written in 1945 in a spirit of holy wrath against the criminals who five years earlier had unleashed the most terrible war in history. At the time the armed forces of the Big Three — the United States, Britain and the Soviet Union — were spread across three continents and the use of the kind of measures outlined in Chapter VII was commonplace. It was assumed, as Article 45 states, that "in order to enable the UN to take urgent military measures, members shall hold immediately available national air force contingence for combined international enforcement action."

Today, Chapter VII has an archaic ring, like the earlier parts of the Old Testament. The enforcement function of the UN has become like an organ withered from atrophy. When the Iraqi army invaded Kuwait, no UN force was available to hit back. It took six months to put in place a force strong enough to confront the aggressor. In the meantime the sanctions ordered against Iraq were causing economic damage to a wide circle of innocent bystanders. The possibility of such effects had been anticipated in the Charter which, in article 50, states that a country "which finds itself confronted with special economic problems rising from the carrying out of enforcement measures shall have the right to consult the Security Council with regard to a solution of those problems." But no one had foreseen the severity and scope of the dislocations that the use of economic sanctions can cause in today's circumstances of interdependence between states. The countries hardest hit by the rise in the price of oil were the poorest nations of the world, as well as the former European satellites of the Soviet Union. India, Pakistan, Jordan, Egypt and the Palestinians in the West Bank and Gaza suffered heavy losses because remittances from their citizens working in Kuwait have stopped. Iraq's many foreign creditors are unable to collect the money due to them.

The overpowering influence of the media adds another unforeseen and unpredictable dimension to the crisis. The drafters of Chapter VII could not have imagined that the preparations for an enforcement action would be carried out amidst a continuous public debate on every military, legal and moral aspect of the complex enterprise. Experts were counting in advance the number of Americans likely to be killed, bishops wrote open letters expressing their moral scruples, members of Congress calculated the domestic political effects of each presidential move. The aggressor himself could not only listen in and record each note of doubt, hesitation and dissent, but also join the debate by addressing the world public via satellite television.

The effect of this agonizing process of public decisionmaking was to blur the moral issue. As the crime committed by Iraq receded in time, the focus of the debate shifted to the question of whether or not it was morally right for the United States and its allies to take military action. Some of the opponents of such action seemed to apply George Bernhard Shaw's dictum: Never strike a child except in anger. With the passage of time the act of punishment was made to appear a cold-blooded attack by a big power against a small country.

The moral aspect aside, those who favored giving economic sanctions more time had a perfectly reasonable case to make. Military experts as well as respected authorities on the Middle East warned that a military intervention could lead to a protracted campaign causing heavy American casualties and possibly uncontrollable upheavals in the Arab world. As it happened, the first casualty of the Gulf war, in the United States as well as in Europe, was the reputation of most of the experts and commentators.

The swift victory achieved by the forces of the American-led international coalition has been proclaimed a turning point in modern warfare — a stunning demonstration of the effectiveness of new high-tech weaponry. It has understandably bolstered American self-confidence. The doubts and hesitations that preceded the Gulf war have been replaced by a belief in the ability of the United States to deal singlehandedly with any future crisis. Yet political success could not have been achieved without the UN. The Security Council resolutions on the Iraqi aggression were essential for mobilizing the large international coalition for the liberation of Kuwait and for persuading the

United States Congress to support military action. Without the Security Council decision economic sanctions could not be enforced. Had the Soviet Union or China used its veto to block decisions in the Security Council, the United States and its allies could have claimed to act under Article 51 of the Charter which upholds "the inherent right of individual or collective self-defense if an armed attack occurs against a member of the UN." But opposition in America, and particularly in Europe and the Middle East, would have been much greater.

The value of UN services was even more apparent in the aftermath of the military operation. Resolution 687 adopted by the Security Council on April 3, 1991, put Iraq, like a prisoner on parole, under UN supervision for an indefinite period. The UN was instructed to deploy an observer unit to monitor a demilitarized zone between Kuwait and Iraq, to make sure that Iraq destroys all chemical and biological weapons and all ballistic missiles with a range greater than 150 kilometers, as well as all research and production facilities for such weapons, and desists from any attempt to produce nuclear weapons. The UN was also put in charge of the fund to be financed by a percentage of Iraq's oil exports to pay compensation for damage caused by the Iraqi aggression. In addition, supervision of remaining economic sanctions will continue to be a UN responsibility.

To say that placing a sovereign state under a UN-run supervisory regime is unprecedented is an understatement; nothing like this has ever before been even contemplated. Legal justification can be found in Article 39 which states that, once an aggression has taken place, the Security Council shall decide what measures shall be taken "to maintain or restore international peace and security." This wording could have been interpreted to cover further action to protect the Kurds and the Shi'ite minority, or even to remove Saddam Hussein from power. The reason why this was not done was that the United States and its allies did not want to endanger the future integrity of the Iraqi state. An intervention on behalf of the Kurds would have upset two members of the international coalition, Turkey and Syria, as well as Iran and the Soviet Union, none of which is prepared to grant autonomy to its own Kurdish minority. By continuing military action beyond the liberation of Kuwait and the imposition of strict limitations on Iraq's war-making capabilities the United States would have risked splitting the coalition and being left with an open-ended responsibility with regard to the future of Iraq. Stability in the Middle East would have been further undermined.

In terms of Realpolitik, the U.S. policy cannot be faulted. But the strong public reaction to the plight of the Kurds revealed once again how difficult it is for governments of open societies to practice Realpolitik in the traditional sense. The massacre of the Kurds in 1975 was hardly noticed by Western opinion; in 1991, the media made sure their fate could no longer be ignored. Western governments were forced to undertake a humanitarian intervention on their behalf. While no government made any commitment to support the Kurds' demand for national self-determination, the fact that the Security Council agreed to consider the case of the Kurds as a matter affecting international security was one more step away from a strict adherence to the doctrine of non-interference in the internal affairs of states.

For the UN, the Gulf war and its aftermath was a watershed event. Whatever the UN will do in a future crisis will be measured against its performance in the case of Iraq v. Kuwait. True, the Security Council does not make decisions in accordance with precedents, like a court of law. Precedents are useful arguments in debate, but each case is decided in the light of prevailing political interests. It is therefore extravagant to claim, as President George Bush has, that the collective action taken against Iraq by itself creates a new world order in which would-be aggressors will be deterred by the fear of having to face General Schwarzkopf and his high-tech forces. But it did show that, given a favorable political constellation, the UN can be used effectively to resist aggression and restore peace. This example will encourage governments to try again. It is, above all, an incentive to reexamine the existing UN collective security system and to make an effort to modernize it.

II

INTERNATIONAL SECURITY
IN THE 1990S

For the past 45 years, the relationship between the United States and the Soviet Union has been the main axis around which the UN has revolved. It has, above all, determined the extent to which it has been possible to use the UN for its primary purpose — the maintenance of international peace and security. The other three permanent members of the Security Council — Britain, China and France — have played a secondary or supportive role; none has been able either to lead or to block action. For historical reasons, and by virtue of their enormous military capabilities, the United States and the Soviet Union continue, at least for the time being, to wield a kind of joint veto over the future of the UN: without an understanding between them the UN cannot work effectively.

This has been demonstrated once again in the Persian Gulf crisis. But an understanding between the two, while necessary, is no longer enough, since of the five states which in 1945 reserved for themselves permanent seats on the Security Council and the right to veto any proposal of substantive matters, only the United States retains the world-wide leadership role which originally justified their privileged position. Yet even the United States lacks the material resources, as well as the political will, to carry the burden of world policeman alone. After a period of unilateralism under President Reagan, the United States under George Bush insists on burden-sharing. But the other four permanent members are unable to share any substantial part of the burden. The Soviet Union needs massive economic assistance to keep its head above water; China, too, faces an uncertain economic future. Britain and France are grappling with mounting economic difficulties. The Big Five are no longer capable of discharging the responsibilities they assumed in 1945.

What still makes the five permanent members more equal than other states in an organization based, in the words of its Charter, on "the principle of the sovereign equality of all its members", is that they are the only ones which possess nuclear weapons or, more accurately, admit to possessing such weapons. (Covert possession by one or two additional states cannot be ruled out.) This puts an extra weight on these five states to act responsibly in their international conduct, but in terms of political influence, the possession of a weapon intended never to be used is an asset yielding diminishing returns. The mystic value attached to nuclear weapons as a symbol of power is bound to go down as nuclear disarmament proceeds and the role of nuclear weapons in superpower strategy is reduced.

The UN collective security system, as outlined in Chapter VII of the Charter, not only lacks the physical means needed for swift action to meet an aggression, it also suffers from what might be called a moral deficit. The legitimacy of the Security Council acting as a supranational body with war-making powers is derived from the military victory achieved by the five permanent members in the second world war over the evil forces of Hitlerism. But the moral authority of the five powers to act as world policemen has been gradually eroded by the events of the past 45 years. Their own conduct hardly inspires confidence in their will to uphold the principles of the Charter. An order based on agreement between, say, a Nixon, a Brehznev and a Mao Zedong may ensure relative stability and peace, but it is not necessarily the kind of order envisaged in the Charter.

The decisions of the Security Council carry great weight because of the power behind them, but it must be born in mind that they reflect the national interests of the permanent members and are not necessarily morally superior to a dissenting view held by a small state determined to defend its national interest.

The mandate the five permanent members acquired in San Francisco in 1945 has been worn out and lost its validity. The Security Council must be revitalized and relegitimized; its composition must be brought up-to-date. This was last done in 1965, when the number of non-permanent members was increased from six to ten in order to accommodate representatives of the newly independent states in the Third World. It would be logical now to reexamine the composition of the Council in the light of the changes in power relations and international priorities that have taken place in the past quarter century.

A reconstruction of the Council requires an amendment to the Charter which must be approved by the permanent members of the Council as well as by two-thirds of all member states. It is unrealistic to assume that any one of the five might allow itself to be voted out of its seat. Each will defend its privileged position by its veto. A change in the composition of the Council can thus be carried out only with the consent of the present establishment.

This should not deter would-be reformers. The case for enlarging the circle of permanent members will be hard to refute. Barring a cataclysmic break-down of the international order, economic power will carry more influence than military power in shaping the world in the 1990s. Even in the Persian Gulf crisis, held up as an example of the continuing importance of military power, economic issues played a key role in the chain of events leading up to the aggression as well as in the Security Council's response to it. To find countries able to share the burden of its military intervention United States had to reach outside of the Security Council, to Japan and Germany.

Burden-sharing must lead to power-sharing or, more accurately, to responsibility-sharing. Surely the time has come to recognize the extraordinary rise of the two former enemy nations of the UN, Japan and Germany, from defeat and occupation to economic preeminence, and to invite them to join the victors of the second world war as permanent members of the Security Council.

The nature of economic power in today's highly integrated world economy is very different from what it was in earlier periods of greater national autarchy, when it could be used by ruthless governments as a means of political pressure to subjugate weaker neighbors. Today no country can succeed, in economic terms, if its neighbors and trading partners fail. The economic power of countries like Japan and Germany must therefore be used to promote a healthy development of the world economy. Both depend on a peaceful and stable international environment. Being peculiarly vulnerable to any break-down in the international order, they have a vested interest in the maintenance of international security. They are thus singularly well qualified to serve on the Security Council.

Until now the Japanese and the Germans have kept a rather low profile in the UN. Their past has inhibited them from providing military personnel for peacekeeping. But as a new generation with no personal involvement in past crimes is taking over, both nations are beginning to reassert themselves. Neither of the two economic giants is content to remain a political pygmy. Each already plays a key role within its own region. Both should be brought into more active participation in the management of international relations as a whole.

The arguments in favor of giving Japan a permanent seat on the Security Council are overwhelming. Japan is already the world's biggest creditor and provider of financial assistance. As second largest stockholder after the United States in the World Bank, Japan has gained the appointment of a Japanese official to one of the two posts of executive vice-president and has begun quietly to lobby for its candidate for the top job at the International Monetary Fund. In the IMF, Japan and Germany now have an equal number of shares, making them coequals behind the United States, while France and Britain have dropped into third rank. In the UN, too, Japan is preparing for a bigger role. It has increased its financial contributions to peacekeeping operations and has begun to prepare its citizens for the possibility of dispatching military units overseas for UN service. Understandably, the Japanese government is demanding to be heard in negotiations on regional conflicts. "The outdated image of Japan is that of a good-natured grandfather living far away," a spokesman for Japanese foreign ministry said recently. "The old approach to us was that when the superpowers had agreed on something, the bill was sent to us. But this is no longer appropriate."

A permanent German seat on the Council is bound to be a more controversial idea. The proponents of "equitable geographical distribution", will no doubt point out that the European Community which aspires to speak with one voice on world affairs already has two permanent seats. The fact is, however, that the EC does not yet have a common foreign policy. In any case Germany should be admitted — not as a regional representative, but as the world's third largest economic power. Its influence extends beyond Europe, in the same way as Britain and France play wider roles by virtue of their cultural and intellectual position of leadership.

In addition to Japan and Germany, India should be considered a potential candidate for a permanent seat on the Council. Its role in the UN in the 1990s is likely to be very different from what it used to be in the days of Jahawarlal Nehru and Indira Gandhi, who claimed to speak for the non-aligned world in the name of a higher international morality. With the change in East-West relations non-alignment and ideological neutralism have become irrelevant. India's new rulers no longer preach morality to the superpowers. Instead, India has moved toward a market economy and has emerged as a regional superpower. Having earlier demonstrated the capacity to produce nuclear weapons, India successfully tested a medium-range ballistic missile in May 1989, thereby joining the exclusive club of countries that have developed the ability both to build a nuclear weapon and deliver it over long distances. (In addition to the five permanent members of the Security Council, they include Israel, Brazil, and Argentina.) The Indian missile, code-named Agni, the Hindi word for fire, has a range of 1500 miles and thus could reach all of Pakistan and other South Asian nations, as well as Afghanistan and areas of Iran and China. According to a high Indian official, "India is headed into the 1990s determined to be self-reliant in all major weapon systems — tanks, planes, missiles." Mahatma Gandhi may turn in his grave, but such are the realities of world politics that, thanks to its military build-up, India now is listened to with greater respect than before. The growing importance of Asia in the world economy is enough justification for elevating Japan and India to the rank of permanent members of the Security Council. But there is also a darker side to the Asian situation which makes it all the more urgent to include the two powers among those primarily responsible for the maintenance of international peace and security. In contrast to Europe, Asia is an uncharted mine field of acute or latent conflicts touching upon the interests of five major powers — the Soviet Union, China, Japan, the United States and India.

It is safe to predict that the Korean question will be high on the international security agenda in the 1990s. The future of Taiwan is uncertain. The issue of Japan's Northern Territories — the four islands Japan claims were illegally occupied by the Soviet Union at the end of the second world war — is still unsettled. China's territorial claims on large parts of Soviet Asia have been set aside but not abandoned. The conflict in Cambodia has not yet been ended. Civil war rages in Afghanistan. Tension between India and Pakistan persists. Internal instability in the Philippines and Indonesia could spill over into international crises.

The lines between the interests of the major powers in Asia are ambiguous or fluid. The idea floated by Moscow of convening an Asian conference on security and cooperation modeled on the Helsinki conference of 1975 has not taken hold so far. But in some form, diplomatic efforts will be made to clarify the relations between the major powers in Asia. There are thus strong reasons for taking steps to strengthen the capacity of the Security Council to deal effectively with Asian issues.

A proposal to make two Asian powers permanent members of the Security Council is bound to provoke demands for permanent seats for Latin American and African states as well. The ambitions of Brazil and Argentina, both potential producers of nuclear weapons, are well known, and their present debt-ridden state is not likely to deter their governments from seeking the coveted status of a permanent member. Among African states, Nigeria is usually mentioned as a possible candidate.

An enlargement of the circle of permanent members would in turn inevitably lead to demands for an increase of the number of non-permanent members. As a result of the complex bargaining process required to change the composition of any major UN organ, the Security Council would probably have to be enlarged to ten permanent and fifteen non-permanent members, instead of five and ten as present.

Such a body would obviously be more unwieldy than the present fifteen-member Council, which is an argument often used by the present holders of permanent seats against making any change at all. But since power itself is now more widely dispersed, reality itself has become more unwieldy. By clinging to the cozy familiarity of the present structure the Security Council weakens its ability to cope with the world as it is.

A proposal to increase the number of permanent members of the Council would set in motion an intense debate on the question of the veto. Must each new permanent member have one or should there be two classes of permanent members — a deluxe class with veto power and a simple first class without it? Perhaps a new system of weighted voting could be worked out.

Such questions open up fascinating vistas of scholastic wrangling among the experts of UN procedure. Governments seek prestige, and the veto is the status symbol to beat all others. In the UN mythology the veto is an evil spell that reduces the UN to impotence or a magic shield that protects the righteous. In reality, it was not the Soviet veto that stopped the UN from rescuing Hungary in 1956; it was military power that stood in the way. But the veto did stop the Security Council from taking a decision it could not have carried out. In the case of the Korean war, the absence of the Soviet representative from the crucial Security Council meeting enabled the United States to wrap its military intervention on behalf of South Korea in the blue-white flag of the UN, but had the Soviet representative been present and cast his veto the United States would have acted any way — under the Stars and Stripes. In more recent instances, the United States has used its veto to defeat anti-Israel resolutions in order to demonstrate its loyalty to an ally, while Britain has used it to serve notice that she is not prepared to join in economic sanctions against South Africa. The veto acts as an anchor that keeps the UN from drifting too far from reality.

In the real world every independent nation has the power of veto; it is inherent in sovereignty. Outside the UN building majority rule does not apply. As the moral certainties of the period of ideological confrontation are being replaced by a more relativist view of the nature of international conflicts, the Security Council is beginning to function in a more subtle manner in dealing with the complexities and ambiguities of regional conflicts. Instead of indulging in public debates and futile voting battles, its members are more inclined to seek consensus behind closed doors; instead of issuing resolutions which deplore, condemn, and demand, the Council uses the quiet diplomacy of persuasion; instead of trying to impose solutions, it promotes negotiating processes between parties to a conflict. The veto is still there, but like nuclear weapons — a deterrent not to be used.

A change in the composition of the Security Council will also necessitate a reappraisal of the functions of the Military Staff Committee. In the original design the MSC was supposed to act as the high command of joint military operations under the UN flag. Such a role is hardly feasible in today's world. It would presuppose a complete identity of interests between the permanent members in a collective military action against an aggressor. This is not likely to happen in the real world.

The Persian Gulf crisis is a case in point. All five permanent members agreed that an aggression had taken place and that its victim had to be liberated, but when it came to going to war, their national interests varied. China opposed military action, but refrained from blocking a decision in the Council. The Soviet Union voted in favor of the resolution endorsing the use of force, but did not send its own armed forces to the Gulf. France joined the military operation only after some hesitation. In these circumstances it would have been inconceivable for the US president to place American forces under the command of a committee of the five powers. By authorizing the United States and its allies to use force the Council made it possible to achieve the goal all five had agreed on without letting differences over means stand in the way. This flexible approach may well serve as an example in future crisis.

The MSC can still have a valuable function as an advisory body and a channel for consultations on military matters. Since the Council is likely to deal mainly with conflicts in the Third World, the usefulness of the MSC would be enhanced through the addition of officers from Japan, India and Brazil.

From Peacekeeping to Peacemaking

The functioning of the Security Council is shaped by prevailing perceptions of the state of international security. Now that the threat of a nuclear war between the superpowers has faded away, the Security Council has been able to deal effectively with several regional conflicts. But the end of the cold war may also have less desirable consequences. Once the link between local or regional conflicts and the sensitive balance between the superpowers has been broken, the major powers may lose interest in areas which, unlike the Persian Gulf, lack vital strategic or economic importance. The burst of activity in the Security Council in recent years may not be sustained for long. The purpose of many of its efforts has been to unburden the American-Soviet agenda by removing from it a number of regional issues, without necessarily trying to settle those issues themselves. The Afghanistan war is a case in point: the withdrawal of Soviet forces had a profound effect on US--Soviet relations, but the internal war in Afghanistan goes on. The real test of the willingness of the major powers to use the Security Council actively as an agency for collective security still lies ahead.

The end of the cold war has not meant an end to conflicts. According to SIPRI, major armed conflicts were waged in 32 different locations in 1989, down by only three from the year before. In addition to major conflicts, SIPRI estimates that there are more than 75 other conflicts which had not resulted in heavy casualties, but were still significant.

Very few of these hostilities are on the agenda of the Security Council or any other UN body. Most are internal wars fought over control of government. But even in the case of disputes between two or more states governments usually turn to the UN as a last resort. As a result, the UN agenda tends to read like a list of the chronic ailments of the international community. The UN treatment may not cure them, but often prevents them from getting worse.

The treatment may include the use of the good offices of the Secretary-General or other kinds of mediation, or simply the opportunity to influence public opinion. In exceptional cases it has involved what has become known as peacekeeping — the use of military personnel for non-forceful purposes.

A total of 19 peacekeeping operations have been mounted by the UN so far. As early as 1948, unarmed UN observers were sent to monitor the cease-fire agreements in the Middle East and in Kashmir. Both of these observer groups still exist, although the armistice agreements in the Middle East are no longer operative. Military observers have subsequently been used in Lebanon in 1958, and more recently in Iran and Iraq, in Afghanistan, in Angola and in Central America.

The first UN force was introduced during the Suez crisis in 1956 to separate Israeli and Egyptian forces. The force set up in Cyprus in 1964 continues to act as a buffer between the Turkish and Greek communities. After the 1973 Middle East war a UN force was instrumental in helping to carry out the disengagement agreements which led to Israel's complete withdrawal from Sinai and the 1979 Egypt-Israel peace treaty. In the Golan Heights, a UN force continues to supervise the separation of Syrian and Israeli forces. The ongoing peacekeeping operation in southern Lebanon, which was established in 1978, has constant difficulties in performing its functions in an area where no government exercises real authority. Now a new operation has been started along the border between Kuwait and Iraq.

In all these cases peacekeeping operations have been designed to stabilize a conflict situation and facilitate negotiations between the parties to a dispute. It has not always had the desired effect. In some cases the presence of the blue helmets has reduced the incentive to compromise and thus helped to freeze the status quo. But it can be argued that this is still better than the alternative of letting the parties fight it out to the finish.

In the last several years, the Security Council has taken the first tentative steps from peacekeeping toward peacemaking by developing a more imaginative and dynamic UN diplomacy for either solving conflicts or preventing disputes from reaching a violent stage. In Namibia the UN engaged in nationbuilding — the first since the Congo operation in the early 1960s. The UN Transition Assistance Group consisting of 8,000 men and women, both soldiers and civilians, guided the former colony of South West Africa onto the road of independence and democracy. In Central America the UN has become involved in a variety of tasks. An observer mission monitored the preparation and holding of elections in Nicaragua in February 1990, the first such operation organized and conducted by the Organization internally in a member state. The UN also played a key role in the voluntary demobilization of the members of Nicaraguan resistance, the Contras. A UN observer group is further engaged to verify the compliance by five Central American governments with their security commitments under a treaty signed by them. The UN is also involved in negotiations to end the internal conflicts in El Salvador and Guatemala and to promote a democratization of society in these countries. Another UN peacemaking attempt involves the plan to resolve the problem of Western Sahara which for years has been fought over between Morocco and the Polisario movement. And the most ambitious project of all is the plan for a comprehensive political settlement of the Cambodian conflict to be carried out under UN supervision and control.

The growing demand for ever more complex and sophisticated services is putting an intolerable strain on the Organization's resources. The total annual cost of current peacekeeping operations is roughly equal to the expenditures in the entire regular budget — almost one billion dollars. It is a modest sum compared to the cost of the conflicts the UN operations are designed to stop. Nevertheless, many governments are slow in paying their share. Unpaid arrears amount to two-thirds of the total cost of peacekeeping. As a consequence, the UN has been unable to pay full compensation to the governments that have placed troops at its disposal. (One third of the troops presently engaged are supplied by four Nordic countries — Denmark, Finland, Norway and Sweden — each of which maintains stand-by forces for use in UN operations and provides special training for peacekeeping units on a regular basis.)

In spite of its high visibility, peacekeeping has been treated like a neglected stepchild among UN programs. The fact that the concept was long considered unconstitutional by the Soviet Union meant that it was conducted by the secretariat as a kind of ad hoc extra-curricular activity. Each new operation had to be improvised from scratch and maintained on a hand-to-mouth basis. Former Undersecretary-General Brian Urquhart has compared the UN operations to "a sheriff's posse mustered at the last minute to prevent the worst."

Now this is changing. The constitutional dispute has been set aside. Moscow has become the chief source of new ideas for improving the UN capacity to fulfill its peacekeeping and peacemaking functions. Some are actually old ideas in modern dress. Thus Soviet representatives have suggested that the Military Staff Committee be activated to plan and prepare peacekeeping operations and that American and Soviet troops also be used in UN service. Until now, no troops of the two superpowers have been used in peacekeeping operations, although logistic support and military observers and staff officers have been accepted.

The participation of officers of all five permanent members of the Security Council in the Kuwait-Iraq observer corps may be seen as a step toward using troops from these countries in UN service. It can be argued that this would enhance the authority of a UN force and ensure the continued support of both superpowers for it. Maybe in the future this will be possible. But under present circumstances a direct and substantial involvement of the two powers in a UN operation would inevitably compromise the basic idea of peacekeeping as a disinterested service to the parties in a conflict and blur the line between enforcement action and the peaceful settlement of disputes. The two powers would be suspected, rightly or wrongly, of pursuing their own strategic or ideological interests in the region; an additional layer of potential friction would be superimposed upon the local conflict. The presence of US and Soviet forces might even draw fire rather than quell it, as was shown by the tragic fate of the American Marines in Beirut. In contrast, a peacekeeping operation under the command of the Secretary-General, using troops from countries with no direct national interest in the critical area, can provide what Dag Hammarskjöld once called "the detached element" needed to stabilize the situation.

That the Secretary-General can act only under the authority and supervision of the Security Council is today taken for granted by all sides; the Soviets need not fear they could be shut out again. It should therefore be possible at last to reach agreement on the principles and guidelines to be observed in peacekeeping operations — a subject that has been dissected from every conceivable angle by a committee of the General Assembly ever since 1965.

The rules will have to be flexible. Each conflict brought before the UN is unique; each operation has to be tailor-made to fit the case in hand. But a great deal can be done to enhance the overall preparedness of the UN to respond to a call for assistance. Stand-by forces trained and equipped for UN service could be created in many more countries in different parts of the world: unified training programs and staff procedures are needed; standardized equipment would be a great advantage. Up-to-date surveillance, communication and information gathering technologies should be adapted for use by peacekeeping forces. As has been pointed out by the International Institute for Strategic Studies in its Strategic Survey 1988–89, "The increasing sophistication of weaponry on the modern battlefield places greater demands on the peacekeeper. The debris in a recently active war zone will be dangerous, the ground dotted with indiscriminately sown mines. In addition, there may be residually active chemicals. To survive, operate and move freely, the peacekeeper will have to be better trained and more comprehensively equipped than at present."[1] In such matters the Military Staff Committee could indeed be useful, provided its place in the overall scheme of peacekeeping is clearly defined; the authority of the Secretary-General must not be compromised.

What the Secretary-General urgently needs is more money. Before he can even dream of acquiring the more sophisticated equipment available to those who make war, he must be able to pay for the ongoing peacekeeping operations. It seems perverse that peacekeeping, the primary function of the UN, has to depend, like a charitable activity, on voluntary contributions of various kinds, instead of being paid for like regular UN programs on the basis of the collective financial responsibility of member states. This is of course due to the controversial past of peacekeeping. Now that its legitimacy and vital importance been acknowledged by all the major powers it is reasonable to expect that its financial foundation will be secured. In addition to the money needed to run current operations, the Secretary-General should have at his disposal an adequate contingency fund to enable him to start new operations promptly. In a critical situation any delay in getting the men in the blue helmets to the scene of the conflict can have grave consequences.

Apart from administrative and technical problems, the new generation of peacekeeping operations raise fundamental issues of principle. UN activities in Central America as well as the peace plan for Cambodia cross the line dividing the foreign relations and the domestic affairs of states. It has indeed become, as President Kennedy once pointed out, a line drawn in water. Until the Gulf war, the UN has become involved in the internal matters of states only with the consent of the governments concerned. The consent of the parties involved in a conflict to the establishment of the operation, to its mandate, to its composition and to its appointed commanding officer, has been considered an indispensable precondition for UN peacekeeping. So is the non-use of force except in the last resort in self-defense.

The cease-fire arrangements in Iraq represent a departure from these principles. The peacekeeping force established to monitor the cease-fire was imposed on Iraq: Baghdad was not consulted in advance. But then the Security Council acted in this case under Chapter VII of the Charter which empowers it to enforce its decisions. The Gulf war has revealed the need for preventive diplomacy. Instead of reacting to violent events or responding to requests for help from member states under attack, it should preempt conflicts and defuse dangerous situations created "by internal socio-economic and other causes," as Soviet Deputy Foreign Minister Vladimir Petrovsky has put it.

A more active preventive diplomacy was already envisaged by the UN Charter, Petrovsky points out. But the Charter at present is like a "sleeping beauty" which must be awakened. How would preventive diplomacy work in practice? "Lets take country. X," Petrovsky postulates. "Lets say the military political situation in it is complex and a serious conflict is impending. The Secretary-General sends his representatives there — objective people who meet with different sides and collect and analyze the information. The Secretary-General has the right to make recommendations on the basis of their report. The Security Council goes into session and works out the measures that would help avert the conflict. All conciliatory measures are used . . ."

Situations in which tension is created by "internal socio-economic and other causes" exist today in many parts of the world, some of them very close to where Mr. Petrovsky is residing. The permanent members of the Security Council, however, would remain outside the scope of UN surveillance. This is implied in the Soviet statement supporting the Secretary-General's proposal for the establishment of a "war prevention center." Such a center, the statement says, "could facilitate a constant exchange of information between UN headquarters and the capitals of the permanent members of the Security Council as well as the chairman of the non-aligned movement." The permanent members, while no longer acting as policemen, would become the benevolent guardians of the unruly smaller states.

A more active role of the Security Council can only evolve gradually and pragmatically, case by case, as indeed peacekeeping has evolved over more than three decades. The way the Security Council has been dealing with the Cambodian question illustrates both the possibilities offered by a more sophisticated approach and the immense problems it may encounter. After a preliminary process of negotiations involving 19 countries, the five permanent members of the Council held six meetings in Paris and New York during 1990 at the vice-ministerial level. They attempted to define the key elements of a comprehensive political settlement of the Cambodia conflict based on an enhanced UN role. Ultimately, the objective is to enable the Cambodian people to determine their own political future through free and fair elections, organized and conducted by the UN, in a neutral political environment. The four rival Cambodian factions were invited to form a supreme national council to implement the peace plan in cooperation with a UN transitional authority including a military as well as a civilian component. The UN operation will in effect administer the country until the new political system has produced a national government capable of taking over.

The fact that thus so far the Cambodian peace plan has not yet been implemented does not invalidate this new method of collective diplomacy. Rather, it tells us something of present day international conditions. The failure so far of the combined efforts of the United States, the Soviet Union, China, Britain, France, Japan, Australia, and other states to persuade the warring factions in a primitive small Asian country to stop fighting and construct a viable government is indeed a striking illustration of the limits of power. It is also an example of the moral dilemma the UN faces when dealing with regional conflicts. The Cambodian people, according to a statement by Secretary of State James Baker, "may be forced to choose between being eaten by a tiger or devoured by a crocodile" — that is, between Pol Pot with his record of genocide, and Hun Sen, a puppet of the Vietnamese aggressor. But each of the five permanent members of the Security Council engaged in the effort to mediate between the tiger and the crocodile could also be identified with a vicious animal. Each has been guilty of acts of aggression against small nations, even against Cambodia itself. Thus the five could not conceivably claim the authority under the Charter to use force collectively to impose a settlement. They have the physical power but lack the moral authority. The case of Cambodia teaches us to be modest and patient in our expectations of what the Security Council is able to achieve.

The UN might learn something from the experience of the Conference on Security and Cooperation in Europe (CSCE). It will continue to be a "process" of regular meetings: high officials will meet twice a year, foreign ministers at least once a year, heads of state and government every other year. But the CSCE now also has a fixed address. A small secretariat — secretariats are always small in the beginning — has been set up in Prague: a Christmas gift for Vaclav Havel who has come to personify the peaceful revolution in Eastern and Central Europe. A center for the prevention of conflicts has begun to function in Vienna to supervise the implementation of disarmament agreements and to sound the alarm in the event it detects any unusual military activities. Eventually it may be able to provide mediation and arbitration services. Parliamentarians from CSCE countries will have their own forum, presumably in conjunction with the Council of Europe in Strasbourg, and mechanisms for international supervision of elections will be devised.

The CSCE is not a collective security system in the traditional sense of the term. As Mrs. Thatcher has put it with characteristic bluntness: "NATO is our defense structure. The CSCE is the perpetual political discussion . . ." The insistence of Western Europe to maintain NATO reflects the unchanged geopolitical reality in Europe. Even without the Warsaw Pact the Soviet Union remains a European nuclear power, but without NATO Western Europe would be left without an American military presence and the protection of the American nuclear umbrella. The UN system of collective security could not serve as a model for today's Europe. Which powers should Europeans appoint to act as policemen authorized to maintain law and order — Russia? Germany? To ask the question is to answer it. As long as security is considered in the traditional sense as a military concept — security against armed aggression — the CSCE clearly must be complemented with other arrangements designed to maintain the balance of military power. But the least likely threat Europe faces in the foreseeable future is an attack by the armed forces of one state against another. Security and stability is more likely to be undermined by conflicts between nationalities within multinational states, like the Soviet Union and Yugoslavia, by large-scale migrations across state borders, by ecological catastrophes or by disputes about the treatment of minorities and other human rights violations. In dealing with problems of this kind the traditional mechanisms of collective security are no longer relevant. New forms and methods of conflict prevention will be needed. They will have to go beyond the issues of military security into the complex web of political, economic and social relations between states.

The CSCE in itself represents a novel approach to international cooperation. All participating governments have declared their adherence to multi-party democracy, free elections and market economy. All have accepted common norms of human rights. Procedures have been adopted that enable governments legitimately to intervene in each other's internal affairs whenever human rights have been violated. What this means is that political relations between states are finally catching up with the new realities created by economic integration and the pervasive power of modern communications.

As a global organization, the UN lacks the cultural coherence that underlies the European institution. Nevertheless, in some respects the CSCE could serve as a model for improvements in the functioning of UN bodies, in particular an enlarged Security Council. The CSCE operates on the principle of consensus, it meets normally behind closed doors, and it has managed, at least so far, to keep its bureaucracy to a minimum.

One form of preventive diplomacy is of course disarmament and arms control. UN proceedings under this heading have concentrated on urging the major powers, in particular the United States and the Soviet Union, to reduce their nuclear arsenals: an exercise with little practical effect. The superpowers have conducted their talks on nuclear disarmament or arms control between themselves without taking much notice of the flood of rhetoric emanating from the UN. Once the two have reached agreement, UN forums, particularly the 40-nations Conference on Disarmament in Geneva, have been used to work out multilateral arms control agreements, such as the treaties on nuclear non-proliferation, outer space, partial test ban, environmental modifications, the seabed, and Antarctica.

The two superpowers will continue to keep negotiations on nuclear weapons in their own hands. Also the talks on conventional disarmament in Europe will be continued in the CSCE, outside of the UN framework. Yet the role of the UN in the general field of disarmament and arms control could become much more important than in the past, provided it will be used for dealing with issues it is uniquely qualified to tackle: above all the proliferation of weapons of mass destruction in the Third World — a phenomenon that threatens to increase the stakes in regional conflicts around the world.

More than twenty developing countries have ballistic missile programs, more than a dozen already possess operational ballistic missile forces, and others have ongoing research and development programs. The dangers posed by these weapons is sharpened by the fact that several of the countries with long-range ballistic missiles are also on the suspected list for possession of nuclear weapons.

While nuclear armed missiles are, of course, the most lethal weapons, the effect of chemical weapons carried by missiles into densely populated areas can be almost equally devastating. It has been estimated that 20 Third World countries either possess or are seeking to acquire chemical weapons capabilities. These include Iran, Iraq, Libya, Syria, Egypt, Israel, North Korea, South Korea, Burma, China, Taiwan, Ethiopia, Pakistan, India, and Vietnam: a rogue's gallery of states with a record of involvement in violent action.

An international regime designed to prevent the spread of nuclear weapons already exists in the shape of the Non-Proliferation Treaty. A ban on the development, production, acquisition, possession, transfer or use of chemical weapons is being negotiated at the Geneva Conference on Disarmament. The bilateral accord reached between the United States and the Soviet Union in July 1989 on chemical weapons provides a strong impetus to the Geneva talks. On ballistic missiles, however, no formal negotiations have so far been initiated under UN auspices. Seven Western countries (Britain, Canada, West Germany, France, Italy, Japan, and the United States) have informally established the Missile Technology Control Regime (MTCR). But this attempt to control exports of technologies relevant to the production of ballistic missiles has had a very limited effect. China and the Soviet Union have continued missile exports, and some of the Third World countries themselves — Argentina, Brazil and Israel, for instance — have entered the lucrative missile export market. Only a very widely based international system of control, comparable to those designed to stop nuclear and chemical weapons proliferation, can be effective on ballistic missiles. To establish such a system is clearly a task for the UN.[2]

According to the Charter, the Security Council is "responsible for formulating plans for the establishment of a system for the regulation of armaments," (Article 26). This has remained a dead letter. Now, however, the Council has taken the first step by imposing on Iraq restrictions designed to prevent the country from acquiring or retaining weapons of mass destruction. In doing so the Council has assumed a heavy responsibility for further steps to remove such weapons from the entire Middle East region.

Since the five permanent members between them sold eighty-seven percent of the weapons bought by developing countries in the late 1980s, they should have the means to extend and enforce an effective arms control system. But do they have the political will to act in unison? The Gulf war has finally put an end to the world's fixation on nuclear weapons, but at the same time stimulated a growing interest in high-tech arms. Soviet Defense Minister Marshal Yazov has stated that the entire air defense system of his country has to be reviewed in the light of the lessons of the Gulf war. Pakistan's prime minister said in a speech on March 16 that "Iraq's crushing defeat underscored the need to make his own nation an impregnable fortress to aggressors." In a report issued in April, the Director of US Naval Intelligence, Admiral Thomas A. Brooks, said that the trend among developing nations was toward "increasingly sophisticated military hardware, especially in naval and air forces," regardless of the cost. By the year 2000, the report forecast, nine nations will join the six that now deploy reconnaissance satellites, a technology that gave the West decisive advantage in the Iraq conflict. Secretary of Defense Richard Cheney predicted in a speech on March 31 that fifteen developing countries are likely to acquire a capacity for Scud-type ballistic missiles by year 2000, eight of which would be able to equip the missiles with nuclear warheads. Thirty countries were expected to possess chemical weapons and biological weapons.[3] None of the permanent members of the Security Council has so far shown any reluctance to meet this growing demand for more sophisticated weapons. The White House told Congress in April that it wanted to allow five Middle East allies to buy an eighty billion dollar package of top-drawer weapons, and President Bush has decided to revive export credits for American arms companies to enable them to compete more effectively with European arms exporters. The Chinese are reported to be offering the sale of a new medium range ballistic missile more accurate and reliable than the Soviet made Scuds. The

Soviet Union, too, which is desperately short of manufactured products salable abroad, is likely to continue its arms exports. There is not much time to stop this new round in the race between the arms merchants and the arms controllers.[4]

III

THE MIDDLE EAST TEST

The crucial test of the usefulness of the UN as an instrument for settling conflicts between nations is the Middle East. Once again expectations are rising. People are saying the UN should now finally "solve the Middle East issue." Once again they will be disappointed. I do believe the UN can play a useful role in promoting a peaceful evolution in the region. But that is not what people mean when they speak of a solution. It is important to make clear what the UN can do there, and what it cannot. A detailed account of what the UN has done in the Middle East so far would fill many volumes. More meetings have been held, more speeches made, more resolutions passed, than on any other item on the agenda; more Blue Berets have served in the Middle East than in any other part of the world; more UN money has been spent on Palestinian refugees than on any other single cause. At several critical junctures the proceedings in the UN have had a decisive impact on events in the Middle East; but in some situations the UN has been left on the sidelines; at times, what has taken place in the UN has actually brought harm to the cause of peace. Some useful lessons can be drawn from these varied experiences.

The first lesson is that anyone dealing with the Middle East must live with ambiguity. The region itself defies precise definition. The British Imperial General Staff, viewing the world from London, used to have a Near East Command and a Far East Command, so the Middle East was presumably the area in between. In the UN the term Middle East is used as a code word for the Israel-Arab conflict. The many savage clashes that have been fought among the Arabs themselves have either been ignored in the UN, or were considered under different headings, like the Iran-Iraq war. The massacre of the Palestinians in Jordan in September 1970, Nasser's campaign in Yemen, the Libyan invasions of its neighbors, the Syrian interventions in Lebanon: none of

103

these violent events appeared on the UN agenda. UN proceedings under the heading of the Middle East thus have had the effect of distorting reality by creating an illusion of Arab unity and perpetuating the myth that the Middle East would become region of peace and harmony if only the Arab-Israel conflict could be settled.

Now, thanks to Saddam Hussein, a more comprehensive and thus more realistic view of the Middle East has been forced on the UN. While a formal link between the Iraqi aggression against Kuwait and the Palestinian issue has been rejected by the United States, the Scud missiles exploding in Tel Aviv and Haifa have made the point that a connection does exist: a link between the military capability of a hostile Iraq and the security of Israel. From the first day of the Iraq-Kuwait war the experts have been saying that everything in the region is bound to change. Actually almost everything remains the same. The conflict between Israel and the Palestinians continues, and so do the rivalries between Iran and Iraq, Syria and Egypt; stability in Lebanon and Jordan remains fragile; the economic imbalances within the Arab world have not been reduced, tension between Islam and modernity has been intensified. What has changed is the outsiders' view. Like a flare shot into the night sky to illuminate the battlefield, the Gulf war has thrown a bright light over the Middle East region revealing a political landscape riddled with acute and latent conflicts.

Old UN hands now say we are back to square one: After fighting for more than forty years to undo the General Assembly resolution of November 1947 on the partition of Palestine, some Arabs at last accept a two-state solution.

American-Soviet relations, too, are back to square one. The resolution on partition could be adopted in 1947 by the required two-thirds' majority because the Soviet Union and its allies sided with the United States (thirty-four delegates voted in favor, thirteen against, including all the eleven Muslim states, and ten abstained, including Britain). This American-Soviet "anti-imperialist" coalition held through 1948, while Israel fought successfully — partly with weapons obtained from the Soviet bloc — to repel the attacks of the Arab armies and to extend her territory. In the first half of 1949, Ralph Bunche, the UN mediator, was able to bring about armistice agreements between Israel and its neighbors because the United States had pushed aside Britain as the dominant power in the region and the Soviet Union was not yet prepared to challenge this extension of American influence. In Stalin's eyes, the birth of the state of Israel was a blow to British imperialism; consequently Zionism was a national liberation movement. Very soon he was to initiate a vicious anti-Semitic campaign in the guise of anti-Zionism, while under the influence of the cold war, American policy also shifted in a direction less favorable to Israel. But by that time the Jewish state was firmly established.

Now again the two superpowers are moving closer on the Middle East issue. The Soviet Union has changed its policy toward Israel. Moderate forces in the Arab world are prepared to accept the existence of the Jewish state. A window of opportunity for peace is opening — who knows for how long. Should the UN not seize it to complete the task that forty years ago was left half done?

In the Middle East it has always been that "all is flux, nothing is stationary": we can never step into the same water a second time. Each of the wars fought between Israel and the Arabs since 1948 has not only changed the map of the Middle East and thus created new political, military and economic realities, but has also had a lasting impact on the perceptions of the parties.

The impact of the Suez War on the Arab mind is a case in point. What the Arabs remember is not the advance of the Israeli forces to the Suez Canal, but the powerful pressure exercised by President Eisenhower to force an Israeli withdrawal. The Arabs were relieved of the responsibility to deal with Israel themselves. If the United States could do this once, it could do it again. Yasser Arafat still today calls Israel "America's naughty child," implying it is up to the parent to make his child behave.

On the Israeli side, too, the Suez war had profound consequences. The withdrawal of Israeli troops from Sinai was conditional. One "assumption" was that the UN Emergency Force stationed on the Egyptian side of the border would prevent raids by Arab fedayeens into Israeli territory. Even more important, there was "a US-Israel understanding that the Israeli withdrawal was linked to free passage through Aquaba, and that any armed interference would entitle Israel to rights of self-defense under the UN Charter."[1]

Thus, in 1957, Israel based its security vis-a-vis Egypt on international arrangements instead of territorial conquest. This gave Israel ten years of peace. But the events of 1967 revealed the fragility of UN peacekeeping operations and the unreliability of international guarantees. Israeli faith in security by international arrangements was destroyed. Ever since those who claim that Israel can only depend on its own military strength have had an upper hand.

The history of the Six Day War in June 1967 has been told many times and need not be repeated here. My interest is focused on the massive damage it caused to the UN as an instrument for maintaining international peace and security. It exposed the inability of the Security Council to take constructive action to prevent a war everyone could see coming.

Nasser's demand for the withdrawal of UNEF on May 16, 1967, could be dismissed as a bluff: a show put on for the benefit of the Syrians and the other Arabs who had been taunting Nasser for hiding behind the UN force while Israel was believed to prepare an attack against Syria. But when on May 22 Nasser announced the closing of the Straits of Tiran to Israeli shipping and to all ships carrying strategic material to Israel, he openly challenged Israel to "exercise its inherent right of self-defense." He knew what he was doing. "The Jews threaten war," he declared, "we tell them: welcome. We are ready for war."

The Israeli government sent its Foreign Minister, Abba Eban, to Paris, London, and Washington to cash the promissory notes it had received in 1957. But de Gaulle told Eban France was not bound by promises made by his predecessors. Prime Minister Harold Wilson was more sympathetic, but was not prepared to commit Britain to any action. President Lyndon Johnson talked of an "international naval escort" to be set up by "the maritime powers" to ensure the right of free passage through the Straits of Tiran. But on May 31 Secretary of State Dean Rusk told a congressional committee that the United States was not "at this time planning any separate military activity in the Middle East, but only within the framework of the UN." In practice this meant "no" to Eban. The promises Israel had received in 1957 were worthless.

Eban's report on his failed mission could not have surprised his government. The Israelis know their history, and history is a mass grave of broken promises. Time and again small nations that have based their security on guarantees issued by the big powers have been betrayed and abandoned. Jews know this better than any other people. Red light for Eban in Washington was green light for the Israeli military leaders. On June 1, a government of national unity was formed, with Moshe Dayan as minister of defense and Menachem Begin, former commander of Irgun, as minister without portfolio. Israel could hardly have done more to advertise her intentions, short of announcing the exact date and hour of her strike.

On the other side, too, preparations for war were ostentatiously publicized. King Hussein of Jordan flew to Cairo and placed his armed forces under Egyptian command. The governments of Syria and Iraq announced that their armed forces would also be part of the joint operations against Israel. Even the King of Morocco pledged part of his army for this purpose. If all this was meant to be a mere show without serious intent, as Nasser later suggested, it was a self-defeating performance — a play that failed because the acting was too convincing.

In the UN, there was no doubt about how the play would end. Ralph Bunche, one of the world's leading authorities on Middle East politics, told anyone who cared to listen that war was inevitable. Yet the UN machinery designed to maintain peace was jammed. U Thant proposed a moratorium of two to three weeks to gain a breathing spell, and this was endorsed by the United States. But neither Israel nor Egypt was prepared to accept it, and the Soviet Union ignored it. "We must not dramatize the situation in the Middle East," the Soviet delegate said at the Security Council meeting on May 24. A French proposal to convene a four-power meeting (Britain, France, the Soviet Union, and the United States) failed to receive a response from Moscow.

Yet the Soviet government advised Nasser to refrain from military action. It also made clear that, in view of its own interest in upholding the right of free passage through international waterways, it could not support the Egyptian position on the Straits of Tiran. Why then did Moscow do nothing to stop the war? Soviet passivity must have been based on the assumption that Israel would either back down or be defeated: Egypt had, after all, received a powerful arsenal of modern Soviet weapons. This gross misjudgment by the Soviet leaders prevented the Security Council from taking any constructive action to defuse the situation. The consequences were disastrous for the Arab allies of the Soviet Union. As a result, Soviet influence in the region was severely reduced.

In retrospect, everything that happened in May and June 1967 in the Middle East is usually presented as inevitable. Nasser was a prisoner of Arab rhetoric and could not help acting as he did. Israel had no choice but to strike first. The United States was preoccupied with Vietnam and could not be expected to take on the task of keeping the Straits of Tiran open. The Soviet Union was bound to stand by its Arab clients. U Thant could do no more than he did. The Security Council was paralyzed by the disagreements between the major powers. Who is to blame? None or all.

Was the UN as an institution deficient? Could improvements in its procedures and methods have made a difference? I believe the answer must be no. All the necessary machinery was in place: it was not used; all the information was available: it was misinterpreted or ignored. No institutional improvements could have overcome the forces of irrationality that brought the crisis to boil.

In the spring of 1967 the two superpowers had not yet developed the habit of consultation. Only after the Israeli air force struck on June 5 did the Soviet government make use of the Hot Line between Moscow and Washington. Even then it took the Soviets thirty-six hours to realize what had happened on the ground. All that time the Soviet delegate in the Security Council, Nikolai Fedorenko, continued to insist that no cease-fire could be accepted without a condemnation of Israeli aggression. Hour after hour he hurled invective at the Israeli delegate, Gideon Raphael, who listened calmly, smoking his pipe. He knew that while the debate went on the Israeli forces continued their advance.

Suddenly, in the evening of the second day, the Security Council paused, while Goldberg and Fedorenko withdrew to confer together. When they returned, the decision had been made. The Hot Line had spoken. The governments of the Soviet Union and the United States had decided that the fighting must stop. The Council unanimously adopted a call to the warring parties to cease fire without delay. That was all: no condemnation, no demand for a withdrawal, no conditions whatsoever. The more hotheaded Arabs immediately accused the Soviet Union of betraying its allies. In fact, the Arabs would have had greater cause to criticize the Soviet Union for not trying to stop the war earlier, preferably before it had started.

Yet more opportunities for making peace were to be squandered. On June 8, while the fighting still went on, Goldberg proposed in the Security Council the immediate appointment of a UN mediator to start peace negotiations between Israel and its Arab neighbors. India supported this idea. The moment seemed propitious. The Israelis had not yet established themselves in the territories they had so swiftly occupied. Elder statesman David Ben Gurion urged his countrymen to put peace before territorial gain. On June 19, the Israeli government adopted a peace plan, according to which Israel was prepared, in return for a genuine peace treaty, to withdraw to the prewar border with Egypt, provided that Sinai would be demilitarized and Israel's freedom of navigation in the Straits of Tiran and the Suez Canal would be guaranteed. Israel was also prepared to withdraw to the prewar border with Syria, provided that the Golan Heights were demilitarized. On the West Bank and Gaza further talks were envisaged. It is conceivable that peace talks at that early moment could have brought success.

But the Soviets were not yet ready, and without their backing no UN mediation effort could be launched. Having suffered a heavy loss of prestige through the defeat of its allies, the Soviet Union decided to put on the "sacred drama" of an emergency session of the General Assembly in order to prove their loyalty to the Arab cause. All of the month of July was wasted on this exercise. Once again, the Soviets misjudged the balance of forces. A Soviet proposal branding Israel as an aggressor received only thirty-six votes. A proposal sponsored by the non-aligned group demanding the unconditional withdrawal of Israeli forces received fifty-three votes, and a Latin-American proposal coupling the demand for an Israeli withdrawal with a call to all parties to refrain from the use of force and to respect freedom of navigation in international waterways received fifty-seven votes. Since neither gained the required two-thirds' majority, the special session failed to reach any conclusion at all.

As usual, more important than the public debate were the private talks that went on behind the scenes. Moscow sent its top American expert, ambassador Anatoli Dobrynin, to negotiate with US Ambassador Goldberg. The two men reached a simple deal on trading territory for peace. The Goldberg-Dobrynin formula was for the Arabs to renounce belligerency in return for an Israeli withdrawal from the territories occupied in June 1967. The Egyptians and Jordanians were inclined to accept, but under pressure within the Arab group they finally backed out. Those living at a safe distance from the battlefield were the most militant. The weakness of parliamentary diplomacy as practiced in the UN is that it tends to leave moderation at the mercy of the extremists. Group loyalty smothers the will to compromise. Nevertheless, the Goldberg-Dobrynin deal was a turning-point — not in the relations between Israel and the Arabs, but in the relations between the two superpowers. It was the beginning of a joint American-Soviet effort to pacify the Middle East.

Having failed to defeat Israel with the help of Soviet weapons, the Arab states now turned to the United States for help. They hoped to persuade Washington to "repeat 1957" — to put pressure on Israel to withdraw. But since the Arab states had cut off diplomatic relations with the United States in the heat of the Six Day War, the UN became the principal venue for negotiations. The regular fall session of the General Assembly brought all the principal actors to New York. At that point the Arabs were prepared to accept the Goldberg-Dobrynin formula and thus recognize Israel's right to free passage through the Straits of Tiran. But once again they missed their chance. The price had gone up. Israel was no longer prepared to agree to a total withdrawal. They would not even discuss Jerusalem. They insisted on obtaining "secure borders." The prewar border, in the Israeli view, had not been secure, so it had to be moved further away from Israel's vital centers. The United States and the other Western powers agreed that "minor adjustments" could be made. Thus the issue that had triggered the war — free passage through the Straits of Tiran — receded into the background; it was no longer in dispute. The territorial question was moved up front.

Resolution 242

The negotiations conducted behind the scenes during the General Assembly session were among the most complex in the history of international diplomacy. The representatives of the four major powers — Britain, France, the Soviet Union and the United States — negotiated among themselves, with the Arab states, with Israel, with their own allies, with other key members of the Security Council and more generally with influential delegations belonging to other groups. The Arab representatives met almost nonstop within their own group or various subgroups as well as with a broad range of other delegations. The Israelis, of course, also lobbied widely among the 120 delegations. The main action, however, was between the Americans and the Arabs on the one hand and the Americans and the Israelis on the other. The Arabs urged the Americans to put the heat on Israel, which they did; the question was, how much.

What finally emerged was Resolution 242 which the Security Council unanimously adopted on November 22, 1967. It stated that "the establishment of a just and lasting peace in the Middle East" required the application of two principles: one, withdrawal of Israeli armed forces from territories occupied in June 1967; two, "termination of all claims or states of belligerency and respect for and acknowledgement of the sovereignty, territorial integrity and political independence of every state in the area and their right to live in peace within secure and recognized boundaries free from threats or acts of force." The resolution further affirmed the necessity for guaranteeing freedom of navigation through international waterways in the area, achieving a just settlement of the refugee problem, and guaranteeing the territorial inviolability and political independence of every state in the area through measures including the establishment of demilitarized zones. Last, but not least, it requested the Secretary-General to designate a Special Representative to "maintain contacts with the states concerned in order to promote agreement."

Most accounts of the negotiations leading to the adoption of resolution 242 designate Lord Caradon, the British UN representative, as its chief author. He was indeed one of the most prominent figures in the UN at the time. Caradon, the former Hugh Foot, brother of Michael Foot, the Labour party leader, was a former colonial official who had served as governor of Cyprus, Nigeria and Jamaica. Having run out of colonies to administer, he had dedicated himself to working for a better world through the UN. As a Quaker, he had an idealistic belief in the ultimate victory of peace and brotherhood between men, but he was also a shrewd political operator and brilliant speaker. Caradon certainly was one of the principal actors in the negotiations on 242, but he was not the real author. Anyone who was involved in the negotiations could recognize in the final text the imprint of Arthur Goldberg and his team, including Assistant Secretary Joseph Sisco from the State Department. Both the substance and the language of the resolution could be traced back to the numerous drafts circulated by the US Mission almost from the moment the fighting in the Middle East had come to an end. Wisely, Goldberg kept himself in the background and let others do the running. But 242 was the crowning achievement of his UN career.

Caradon does, however, deserve credit for solving at the last moment what had seemed an insoluble difference blocking unanimity in the Security Council. The Arabs, backed by the Soviet Union and France, insisted on an Israeli withdrawal from all the territories occupied; the Israelis, backed by the United States and Britain, insisted they would only withdraw to "secure borders." How to reconcile "withdrawal from" with "withdrawal to"? Caradon found a way. He proposed to drop the definitive article from the word territories: withdrawal "from territories," not "from the territories." The Soviets did not mind, because Russian does not have a definite article. The French did not mind either, because in French the phrase was still the same. The Israelis stated that their acceptance of the resolution was based on the English text. By adding a touch of ambiguity, like a drop of angostura in a glass of gin, Caradon had made the text palatable to all parties.

Almost exactly fifty years earlier, on November 2, 1917, another British peer, Lord Balfour, had issued that masterpiece of ambiguity — the declaration stating that Britain was in favor of establishing in Palestine "a national home for the Jewish people," while it was "clearly understood that nothing shall be done which may prejudice the civil and religious rights of existing non-Jewish communities in Palestine." The contradiction so deftly built into the Balfour Declaration still remains unresolved, just as the territorial clause of Resolution 242, a much quoted UN document, continues to be subject to conflicting interpretations.

Yet it would be wrong to consider Resolution 242 fatally flawed at birth. At the time it was negotiated the primary objective of the United States was to launch a UN mediator on a course of negotiations between the parties on the basis of principles agreed upon among the major powers. The Caradon amendment made this possible by leaving the territorial issue to be settled in the coming talks.

No importance was attached at the time to the Arab objections to the use of the term "mediator." A Special Representative of the Secretary-General, it was thought, could do the job just as well. The man chosen was Gunnar Jarring, a Swedish diplomat who had previously served as his country's representative in the UN and at the time was ambassador to Moscow. He was the very model of a neutral diplomat, of discretion personified; he was not known for personal initiative or imagination.

Why Jarring? I asked Ralph Bunche at the time. His answer was that Jarring had done a good job as mediator in the Kashmir dispute. But the Kashmir dispute was still unsolved? Yes, said Bunche, but Jarring had never put a foot wrong and retained the full confidence of all parties.

The choice of Jarring meant that the activities of the Special Representative would be firmly controlled from the 38th floor, by Bunche himself. He had been the successful mediator in 1949. But in 1967 he was a sick man, worn down by diabetic ailments.

Great hopes accompanied Jarring on his travels between the capitals of Israel and its neighbors. People living in Western societies are conditioned to believe that any dispute can be settled by a fair and reasonable compromise. If the parties are unable to agree between themselves, a detached arbitrator, an honest broker, will show them the way. But what is fair and reasonable to a cool Swede may seem treason to an Arab or a deadly threat to an Israeli. Jarring soon found that the Arab rejection of the term of mediator was more than a semantic quibble. The Arab summit meeting in Khartoum in August 1967 had issued "three nos": no peace with Israel, no recognition of Israel, no negotiations with Israel concerning any Palestinian territory. In the Arab view, Resolution 242 did not require any further negotiations: it simply had to be implemented. In other words, Israeli forces had to be withdrawn before anything else could happen. There was no need for mediation.

The Israelis were not interested in mediation either. In their view Jarring's job was to bring the parties together and leave them to settle matters between themselves. Real peace, according to the Israeli position, could only be made in face to face talks between the former enemies. Nothing short of that could convince them that the Arabs genuinely were prepared to accept the state of Israel and live with it in peace.

As in the Kashmir case, Jarring never put a foot wrong. For three years he travelled between Israel and the Arab capitals carrying pieces of paper from one government to another. He retained the full confidence of all the parties. But he made no progress toward peace. Then, suddenly, in February 1971, he decided to take the initiative himself.

The opportunity for such a step had been created by the change of leadership in Egypt. Nasser had died in September 1970 and had been replaced by Anwar Sadat. The new Egyptian president was underestimated by virtually everybody. He was regarded as an interim figure. It was not understood that Sadat was from the beginning determined to change the course of Egyptian policy. He abandoned the pan-Arab dream Nasser had pursued at great cost to his own country, and devoted himself to the national interests of Egypt. Recovery of Sinai, the territory lost to Israel, was his priority. If this could not be achieved by war, it had to be done by negotiation. Since the other Arab countries were not prepared to negotiate with Israel, Egypt had to go it alone. On February 4 1971, Sadat told the Egyptian parliament "that if Israel withdrew her forces in Sinai, I would be willing . . . to sign a peace agreement with Israel." He confirmed this in a message to the UN a few days later.

This was a momentous announcement: the first break in the Arab ranks of "three nos." It emboldened the ever cautious Jarring to make his move. Four days after Sadat's speech he sent Israel and Egypt identical letters containing an outline of a peace plan between the two countries. Egypt's reply was positive: Jarring's plan was after all just a dressed-up version of Sadat's own proposals. But the Israeli government refused to agree to a withdrawal to the pre-June 5, 1967, lines. The United States endorsed the Jarring plan, but the Israelis would not budge. And that was the end of the Jarring mission. On March 25, 1971, he returned to Moscow to resume his post as Swedish ambassador. Formally he remained Special Representative, but he never returned to the Middle East.

This chapter in the convoluted history of the Middle East negotiations has received less attention than it deserves. Here was a real opportunity to break the deadlock. Why was not more done? It seems inexplicable that U Thant let Jarring give up at the very moment when a breakthrough seemed possible. But Ralph Bunche had died, and U Thant himself, whose term in office was coming to an end, was suffering from a bleeding ulcer. Besides, the UN peace effort was tied to the concept of a comprehensive settlement as envisaged in Resolution 242: a separate peace between Egypt and Israel was anathema to the other Arabs. The United States, too, made only a feeble effort to back the Sadat initiative. The Middle East was handled by Secretary of State William Rogers, which meant in practice that it had a low priority on the Nixon-Kissinger agenda.

But why did Israel dismiss the Sadat offer in such a high-handed fashion? The Israeli government, according to Conor Cruise O'Brien, was in a state of "apathetic immobility."[2] I happened to visit Israel soon after the Jarring initiative and had a long talk with Prime Minister Golda Meir. She had nothing but contempt for Sadat. She simply did not believe he was serious. In her view Israel had no reason to make any concession whatsoever. As things turned out, Israel paid a heavy price for her arrogance.

Peace with Egypt

Sadat had to take one dramatic step after another before he was taken seriously. In July 1972 he threw the Soviet military advisers out of Egypt. In October 1973 the Egyptian forces crossed the Suez Canal, shattering Israels' complacent confidence in her own invincibility. In

November 1977 Sadat himself flew to Jerusalem to be received by Prime Minister Menachem Begin, the superhawk of Israeli politics. In September 1978 the Camp David Accords were signed in the White House. And finally in March 1979, Sadat was able to sign the peace treaty between Egypt and Israel which in all essentials conformed to what he had proposed eight years earlier.

The failure of the Jarring mission was a setback to the internationalist belief in the use of the UN as the primary instrument for making peace in the region. Perhaps the notion of an honest broker in the Middle East is a contradiction in terms. During Henry Kissinger's spectacular shuttle tour between the Middle East capitals in the summer of 1974, Lord Caradon asked an Arab colleague: "Are you not afraid that Kissinger says one thing in Cairo and another in Jerusalem?" The Arab looked at him pityingly: "But of course he does," he replied.

And of course, Kissinger was not an honest broker or mediator. He was an enforcer of American policy in the Middle East. As such, he was even welcome in Damascus, although the Syrian government had never accepted Resolution 242 and had refused to receive Jarring. Kissinger could back up his art of persuasion with the power of the United States. He could promise material or political support — or threaten to withhold it. Above all, he was free from the constraints of the concept of a comprehensive settlement and the four-power framework.

Nevertheless, Resolution 242 was and remains important. True, it has not been "implemented," as the Arabs would put it, except between Israel and Egypt. But it has served a useful purpose as the expression of an international consensus, enabling the major powers to deal with the Middle East issue on the basis of an agreed framework. East-West relations have been thus effectively insulated from being constantly exposed to shocks from tensions in the Middle East. Still today, Resolution 242 is invoked by governments, like a ritual incantation, whenever the Middle East is discussed.

The Palestinians

Even Henry Kissinger, never a UN fan, found in 1973 that he needed the Security Council and its rituals to put an end to the Yom Kippur war. But the procedure he used was significantly different from the long drawn out process of parliamentary diplomacy employed in 1967. After an exchange of threats, the two superpowers quickly agreed on what had to be done. Kissinger flew to Moscow and worked out the words with General Secretary Leonid Brezhnev. The next day the Security Council accepted the document without a change of comma. This was the high noon of d'tente.

A more substantial difference between 1967 and 1973 was the emergence of the Palestine Liberation Organization as a factor in the Middle East equation. Resolution 242 makes no mention of the Palestinians as a nation: they figure in the text only as refugees. At the time the Resolution was drafted, the price of oil was three dollars per barrel. After the Yom Kippur war, the price rose to ten dollars, and the PLO Chairman, Yasser Arafat, was given presidential treatment in the UN General Assembly.

The character of the Middle East issue in the UN context was changed almost overnight. In 1967 and again in 1973, the issue had been how to stop the fighting and start peace negotiations between states. Now a quite different issue was brought to the forefront: how to satisfy the demand for national self-determination of a stateless people. In principle, the Palestinians had an unassailable case: Why should they be denied what the UN time and again has proclaimed an inalienable right belonging to every people? But the Palestinian claim of self-determination, as it was presented at the time, was coupled with an attempt to delegitimize the State of Israel and expel it from the UN. In Arab rhetoric, justice for the Palestinians implied the destruction of Israel. Although such an implication was rejected by all governments that had recognized Israel, including the Soviet Union and its allies, few except the United States displayed much vigor in defending Israel's right to exist. Even Western Europe, intimidated by oil power, was subdued. In Israeli eyes, the UN became enemy territory; their confidence in UN-sponsored negotiations or UN peace services was shattered. As a result, the UN role in the Middle East was sharply reduced. Peace between Israel and Egypt was negotiated in Camp David, not in the Security Council.

The UN's role in Lebanon has not been very successful either. After the Israeli invasion of South Lebanon in March 1978, the Security Council was still able to agree on establishing a peacekeeping force — the UN Interim Force in Lebanon, UNIFIL — in the hope of persuading Israel to withdraw. In fact, the Israelis never trusted UNIFIL to protect their northern border against Palestinian guerrilla attacks and continued to keep control over Southern Lebanon with the help of Lebanese proxy forces. A year later, the deterioration in American--Soviet relations prevented the Security Council from setting up a UN force to act as a buffer between Israel and Egypt in the Sinai, so a non-UN force, the Multinational Force and Observers (MFO) was created under American auspices. It was deployed in 1982 and still remains in the field. Again, in August 1982, a multinational force made up of American, French, Italian and British troops was formed outside of the UN to evacuate the PLO troops from Beirut. A second multinational force sent to Lebanon with a more open-ended mission was hastily withdrawn in 1984 after suffering heavy casualties in terrorist attacks. Attempts by the Arab League to deploy its own peacekeeping forces in Lebanon have been ineffective or merely served as cover for Syrian military interventions. A French attempt in the spring of 1989 to protect the Christian community in Lebanon against brutal attacks by Syrian forces also ended in failure.

Altogether, the major powers have been unable or unwilling to take effective action, either through the UN or outside of it, to prevent the destruction of Lebanon, a founding member of the UN, as an independent state: a grim warning to all small nations. The fate of Lebanon is all the more tragic in that it can be compared to that of an innocent bystander who is struck down by a stray bullet in a fight between two armed gangs.

The tragedy of Lebanon in the 1980s was the nadir of four decades of UN efforts to achieve peace and stability in the Middle East. Since then the Palestinian uprising, the intifada, and the exodus of Soviet Jews have transformed the region in a manner unforeseen by earlier UN resolutions. Finally, the war in the Persian Gulf has raised hopes of a comprehensive settlement of regional issues.

It is possible, though by no means certain, that in the post-Gulf war period the UN will once again become a more effective instrument for dealing with the situation in the Middle East. The United States will be the dominant player, and it is likely that the United States will need the UN to legitimize the peaceful reconstruction of the region, just as it needed the UN to legitimize its military intervention. Most probably peacekeeping services in a broad sense will continue to be required.

Some things will have to change in the UN, however, before it can again become a central forum for the peace process. The Israelis must regain confidence in the organization as a constructive agency for peace and security. This is well understood among moderate Arab representatives. Several of them have told me privately they wish a way could be found to erase from the UN record the 1975 General Assembly resolution equating Zionism with racism. They do not say this in public and I do not expect it will be done, but there are other ways in which the moderate Arab governments can signal their change of heart. One is to stop hounding Israel out of every UN body. It is one thing to criticize the policies of the government of Israel, quite another to try to delegitimize the Jewish state.

Given the large number of Arab and other Islamic states, the votes in the UN will always be stacked against Israel. As a result Israel appears to act undemocratically by constantly defying the will of the majority, though in fact UN votes reflect the interests of governments, few of which represent democracies.

Another reason for Israel's aversion to the UN as a venue for negotiations on the Middle East is the Soviet veto in the Security Council. Now that Soviet policy has changed this may no longer seem an obstacle. But will the more cooperative Soviet attitude last? The answer depends on one's assessment of the factors underlying Soviet policy in the Middle East.

The new approach adopted by Moscow in the late 1980s can be described as a change of tactics: an overdue response to the changed realities in the Middle East. After the peace treaty between Israel and Egypt and the decline of oil power, Soviet interests could no longer be served by rigid support for the radical Arab states and hostility toward Israel. As a result of the immobilism of the Brezhnev period the Soviet

Union had become isolated and excluded from the mainstream of Middle East politics. Worse still, the continued American-Soviet confrontation on Middle East issue had become an obstacle to Gorbachev's efforts to improve relations with the United States and the West in general. Thus both global and regional interests urgently required a more flexible approach, including the restoration of contact with Israel.

On a deeper level, however, Soviet diplomatic maneuvers in the Middle East touch some of the most sensitive issues raised by Gorbachev's domestic policies. One of them obviously is the position of the Islamic population within the Soviet Union. The risk of revolutionary Islamic fundamentalism spreading from Iran and Afghanistan into the Soviet Asian republics is obvious. Until recently Soviet experts had seemed confident that such influences could be rejected. The Asian peoples living in the Soviet Union had, after all, reached more advanced material and educational standards than their brethren south of the Soviet border: "A higher form of social organization," as the Soviets used to say. In the beginning of the Afghanistan campaign, many Russians genuinely believed they were bringing civilization to a primitive tribal society. But they were repulsed, and now the fundamentalist danger is taken seriously in Moscow. Gorbachev himself alluded to this in a brief comment on the riots in Uzbekistan in June 1989: "I think fundamentalism has bared its teeth." Potentially, fundamentalism is a greater threat to the perestroika than nationalism in the European republics of the Soviet Union, for it rejects the Western model of progress which is at the core of Gorbachev's drive to modernize the country.

The implications for Soviet policy in the Middle East are obvious. By any rational analysis the long-term interests of the Soviet Union are not threatened by Israel or by the United States as much as by continued conflict and chaos which feeds the revolutionary currents in the Islamic world. It follows that the Soviet Union has a genuine interest in helping to stabilize the Middle East region by strengthening the moderate forces in the Arab world.

The question is, however, whether rationality can prevail. In order to be able to conduct a rational policy on the Middle East the Soviet leadership must come to terms with the "Jewish question" and on this it encounters powerful forces of irrationality with deep roots in Russian history.

It is instructive to recall the role played by the Jewish question in the early years of this century. The Russian Finance Minister Count Witte argued in 1900 that "without her own industry Russia cannot achieve genuine economic independence, and the experience of all nations indicates palpably that only countries which enjoy economic independence have also the capacity fully to unfold their political might." But industrialization required Western capital, and to attract Western capital Russia had to liberalize her political system. Witte and his supporters realized that Russia's international standing would be enhanced if her Jewish subjects were granted their civic equality. But proposals to this effect ran into heavy opposition from the conservative bureaucracy and the right-wing politicians who relied on antisemitism as an instrument of policy, and Czar Nicholas himself rejected Witte's plan on grounds of "conscience."

Similarly, Gorbachev realized that an improvement in relations with the United States and the West in general required the removal of restrictions on emigration and an end to discriminatory treatment of Soviet Jews, but once again the more liberal policy has set in motion a strong groundswell of antisemitism. Indeed, the Jewish question has become one of the issues on which the struggle between the modernizers and the traditionalists is being fought. In any assessment of the future course of Soviet policy in the Middle East the influence of the "anti-Jewish vote" must be taken into account.

With this reservation, it is nonetheless possible to assume that in the post-Gulf war situation the Soviet Union will have a genuine interest in promoting stability in the Middle East. This can only be achieved through cooperation with the United States. The Soviet Union is too weak to mount an effective opposition to the United States in the region; it can retain its influence only by adopting a policy of partnership.

The prospect of such a partnership has revived talk of what in UN jargon is called an "imposed settlement" of the Arab-Israel conflict. Indeed, on both sides the moderates long for the two powers to force the hawks to submit to a compromise. But this would be a way for both sides to avoid accepting responsibility for living with whatever settlement may be reached. If there is one thing that can be learned from past experience, it is that a solution reconciling the security of Israel with the national rights of the Palestinians can ultimately be reached only through direct negotiations between the parties themselves. As Sir Anthony Parsons, a former British UN representative, has pointed out, "it is no use expecting outside bodies, including the UN, to draw up detailed blueprints and to impose them on recalcitrant parties to dispute. It simply does not work."

The idea of a partition of the former territory of Palestine enforced by the major powers still lives on in UN circles. In the aftermath of the second world war partition was indeed the favored method of solving international conflicts. Germany, Korea and Vietnam were cut in half along the lines dividing the two rival power blocs; British India was partitioned between Hindus and Muslims; later Cyprus was divided between Greeks and Turks. The results have been unhappy. Vietnam was unified after decades of fighting. In Korea the conflict between North and South remains unsolved. On the Indian subcontinent, partition has been followed by four decades of violence and tension. In Cyprus, UN troops are still needed to watch over a fragile truce between the two communities. And in Northern Ireland, the product of an earlier partition, violence continues to be part of every-day life. In Germany, peace was maintained by the armed forces of the two superpowers facing each other across the dividing line, until in 1989 the collapse of the Communist system opened the way to unification.

The trend in the world today is in the direction of integration, not separation; open borders, not barbed wire, as guarantees of peace and security between nations. As long ago as 1973, Abba Eban, then foreign minister of Israel, pointed out that "the ultimate guarantee of peace (between Israel and its Arab neighbors) lies in the creation of common regional interests in such degree of intensity, such multiplicity of integration, such entanglement of reciprocal advantage, as to put the possibility of war beyond rational contingency." The model he had in mind was the Benelux economic union between Belgium, The Netherlands and Luxembourg, which combines national independence of each component with a large measure of integration and mutual openness.[3]

The trouble is, of course, that the mutual trust taken for granted within the Benelux is lacking between Israel and the Arabs. An example more relevant than idyllic Benelux is what is going on in the Soviet Union: separation must come before integration. Only nations that feel secure in their own independence can allow themselves the luxury of sharing their sovereignty with others.

To dismiss the idea of an imposed settlement is not to dismiss the UN altogether from the Middle East peace process. There are at least three ways in which the UN can be used to promote stability and security in the region. First, the Security Council can serve as a forum for negotiations between the major powers, as it was in 1967, to produce agreement on the general frame of a Middle East settlement. Such an agreement could not by itself solve the issue, but a lack of understanding between the major powers could easily wreck negotiations between the parties themselves.

Second, a vitally important function of the UN in support of a Middle East peace process is to institute effective regional disarmament. Determined and united action by the major powers will be needed to eliminate the threat posed by the existence of nuclear and chemical weapons and long-range missiles in the region. This will require, among other measures, a self-denying solidarity between the major suppliers of modern weapons. Again, the Security Council is a ready-made instrument for diplomatic efforts to this end.

Third, the UN must be prepared to make available to the parties in the Middle East whatever peacemaking or peacekeeping services they might need. Here the Secretary-General plays a key role. Formally, he needs authorization from the Security Council or some other UN body for any official move. He cannot inject himself into a negotiating process without being requested by all the parties to do so. At all times, he must avoid any step that might jeopardize his impartiality in the eyes of any of the parties to the conflict. But behind the scenes the Secretary- General can prod the Security Council to take necessary action. He can undertake, on his own initiative and without formal authorization, factfinding projects and studies anticipating some of the problems of peacekeeping, demilitarization, supervision and verification that are bound to arise. The Secretary-General can also use outside experts. While his political role is circumscribed, he has a great deal of scope for intellectual leadership in the search for peaceful solutions.

IV

THE ECONOMIC AND SOCIAL
DIMENSION

As nowadays practically every meeting between the political leaders of the major powers is billed an historic occasion, a turning point in human affairs or a breakthrough to a better world, the true summits that from time to time are reached in the never-ending flow of consultations between governments may be passed by without due recognition. One such meeting that deserves to be remembered was the one misleadingly called the "Economic Summit" of the heads of state or government of the seven biggest industrial nations — the G-7 — held in Paris in July 1989.

Its importance was not due to great foresight or careful design. The annual reunions of the seven political leaders plus the president of the EC Commission have become part of the routine of world politics. They were started in 1975 by the French President Valéry Giscard d'Estaing and the West German Chancellor Helmut Schmidt in the form of an intimate get-together at which the heads of government, free from the shackles imposed upon them by their advisers, could speak their minds about such things as the dollar and interest rates. But gradually other pressing issues began to intrude, until in the summer of 1989 the G-7 were simply overwhelmed by the problems of the world at large. The economic worries of the rich nations — exchange rates, trade imbalances, inflation — were pushed into the background, and the greater part of the meeting was spent on environmental issues such as global warming, deforestation, chlorolfluorocarbons and oil spills, on the debt crisis, on the plight of Eastern Europe, and on relations with China.

For the first time the G-7 started dealing with a comprehensive agenda of economic and social issues for the 1990s, including the connection between environmental protection and economic development, the effects of hyperinflation on democracy in Latin America, the consequences of the break-up of Stalin's empire, and the growing importance of human rights in relations between states. By doing so the seven leaders transformed, almost inadvertently, their annual meeting into a kind of super-council for global management: not the first time a new institution is born in spontaneous response to the pressure of changing conditions rather than as a product of rational planning. The significance of this was grasped by Gorbachev even before the Seven themselves had quite realized what they had done, as was shown by the surprise letter he dispatched to Paris to solicit an invitation to the next meeting. (He was not admitted to the 1990 meeting in Houston, Texas, and in 1991 the door to the G-7 Club is firmly closed.)

Where does this expanded agenda of the economic summits leave the UN? The priorities of busy politicians speak for themselves: The heads of government of the rich and powerful nations meet at their summits; the ministers of finance and the chiefs of central banks gather at the annual meetings of the International Monetary Fund and the World Bank; the ministers of trade attend the GATT rounds; ministers in charge of economic policy get together at OECD meetings; but at meetings of UN bodies dealing with economic and social questions, including the Economic and Social Council (ECOSOC) itself, only officials of lower rank can be found.

Not so long ago it used to be said that the UN should be judged primarily by its contribution to economic and social progress in the world, rather than by its ability to keep the peace. This claim is not heard today. Indeed, opinion may have swung too far in the opposite direction, unfairly diminishing the UN record in the economic and social sphere.

A study made by the UN Association of the United States of America (UNA) has sought to identify some of the positive achievements of UN activities in the economic and social field. The humanitarian assistance provided by UN agencies to refugees and to victims of disasters and emergencies is an obvious example: here the UN has a near-monopoly. From the host of UN programs designed to promote acceptance of common norms and standards and the adoption of converging national policies on social issues the study singles out two — those on population, and the environment. The UN has clearly influenced world population policy by increasing awareness of the relationship between population, development and the international economic system, by promoting an international consensus among governments in favor of population stability as a goal and by helping many Third World countries to develop policies designed to reach that goal. On the environment, a far-sighted Swedish initiative led to the 1972 UN Conference on the Human Environment held in Stockholm, which "stimulated a dramatic evolution in awareness of environmental risks and triggered the establishment of mechanisms for managing these risks," including the creation of environmental ministries in many countries, the formation of the UN Environment Program (UNEP), and the conclusion of treaties and conventions, among them the accord on protection of stratospheric ozone. The plan to halt pollution in the Mediterranean Sea was also the result of a UN initiative. The UNA study also points to the Third Conference on the Law of the Sea in 1973-1982 as an example of an important global negotiating process successfully carried out under UN auspices. "While some obstacles, such as disagreement on the international seabed authority, are slowing down ratification by signatories, the convention produced by the conference largely succeeded in reconciling an immense array of interests, and many of its provisions regarding the breadth of the territorial seas, passage through straits, fisheries, the exclusive economic zone, the definition of the continental shelf, etc., are widely observed by the world community."[1]

Human Rights

The UN record on human rights is mixed and ambiguous. After the adoption in 1948 of the Universal Declaration on Human Rights, a number of other covenants and instruments on civil, political, economic, and social rights, as well as provisions against genocide, torture, and racial and sexual discrimination, have been adopted. An elaborate institutional machinery has been set up to implement and enforce the human rights standards thus codified.

Since acceptance of the Western liberal values embodied in these standards would fatally undermine many of the regimes represented in the UN, it is not surprising that the enforcement powers of UN human rights bodies have remained feeble. Western opinion has often been outraged by the hypocrisy of UN proceedings on violations of human rights in various parts of the world. Actually, some degree of hypocrisy is inevitable in any intergovernmental organization, even between allies: it is, after all, another name for tact. But in the UN it has often risen above a tolerable level

This is not, however, grounds for dismissing as humbug the whole structure of human rights covenants and implementation machinery created by the UN. It represents in itself a major new development in international relations. In an historical perspective, forty years is a short time for the gap between words and deeds to narrow. As one expert noted,"Having won a revolution in the name of man's inalienable rights, the founding fathers of the United States incorporated slavery into the new nation's constitutional foundations. Seventy--six years passed before formal emancipation. Another century passed before blacks in America could enjoy the full rights of citizenship. The distance the UN has come in four decades is one ground for optimism about where it will go in the next four."[2]

Even Ronald Reagan, at the end of his presidency, relented toward the UN. In his farewell speech to the General Assembly on September 23, 1988, he praised the UN for progress on human rights, referring specifically to the decision of the Human Rights Commission to investigate human rights abuses in Cuba: "A major step toward ending the double standard and cynicism that had characterized too much of its past." He went on to outdo Jimmy Carter in placing the human rights issue at the very top of the international agenda: "It must be a first concern, an issue above others . . . wherever one turns in the world today there is new awareness, a growing passion for human rights."

In many ways, the communications revolution has blurred the line between domestic and foreign affairs. Among nations which share similar values the principle of non-intervention in the internal affairs of other states has been diluted or modified by common consent. The Organization of American States (OAS) has developed methods to expose human rights violations in Latin America; the Human Rights Convention of the Council of Europe makes the individual citizen a subject of international law enabling citizens of member states to take their governments to an international court. The thirty-four states participating in the Conference on Security and Cooperation in Europe (CSCE) have accepted detailed provisions with regard to the practical application of human rights, and created an unprecedented monitoring system enabling governments to check each other's performance and to demand rectification of abuses.

Quite apart from institutional arrangements between governments for dealing with human rights issues, technology has made sure that no country is any longer immune to outside scrutiny. How a government treats its own citizens affects its relations with other states. But international reactions to violations of human rights are highly selective. Systematic oppression practiced in one country causes hardly a ripple of interest, while an isolated act or incident in another becomes a world sensation. No government can plead "not guilty" to the charge that it applies a double standard. What President Roosevelt once said of a Latin American dictator and his misdeeds — "He is a son of a bitch but he is our son of a bitch" — has been repeated in many languages throughout the ages in every major capital.

The double standards still prevail, but in countries where public opinion counts, governments are losing control over human rights policy to the media, leading to a new selectivity dictated by news value. This introduces an arbitrary and unpredictable element into international relations. Access by television camera crews often determines the object of the indignation of Western public opinion at any given moment.

The massacre in Tiananmen Square in Beijing in June 1989 is a case in point. A worse slaughter of student demonstrators in Burma less than a year earlier was quickly forgotten. The cruel persecution of the Kurds, the oppression of the Hungarian minority in Romania, the expulsion of the Turkish minority from Bulgaria — just to mention a few recent cases — have hardly had any political repercussions. But China is a much more important country, the Chinese reform policy had been idealized in the West, and TV cameras were right there on the spot. As a result the United States Congress voted overwhelmingly to impose sanctions against China going well beyond the measures taken by President Bush. One wonders what would have happened to the Nixon-Kissinger grand strategy in the early 1970s had even a small part of the atrocities committed in China during the Cultural Revolution been shown on American television.

Those who deplore the limitations thus placed on the practice of Realpolitik may console themselves with the thought that the attention span of the media is notoriously short. Public indignation cannot be sustained for long unless fed with new shocks at regular intervals. Sanctions tend to wither away, ambassadors dramatically recalled quietly return to their posts: the protesters find new objects.

Internal Matters

Nevertheless, while the influence of human rights issues on relations between states remains superficial and erratic, opinion in Western society will go on harassing governments with demands for morality in foreign policy. The balance between the rights of the individual and the right of national self-determination has clearly tilted in favor of the former. "Only men have rights: The right of national self-determination is a barbaric instrument," proclaimed the headline over a recent article by Ralph Dahrendorff, the German social thinker.[3] This is a typical example of the present tendency to look upon national sovereignty as a license for tyrannical governments to mistreat their own citizens. But only members of wealthy nations whose independence can be taken for granted can afford to hold such a view, and it remains to be seen whether it can survive any severe setback to the prosperity and sense of security at present prevailing in the West. For the majority of mankind, it is still a luxury — caviar for the general. For small, weak, and poor nations the struggle for the right of self-determination has not yet ended. Many peoples are still deprived of the right to govern themselves; many oppressed minorities still lack adequate autonomy. And perverse as it may seem, history shows that many people prefer to be badly governed by their own kind to being efficiently administered by alien rulers.

In the UN, sovereignty will continue to take precedence over other rights. No other course is possible in an organization with a global membership in a divided world. Article 2:7 of the Charter, which prohibits the organization from intervening in matters within the domestic jurisdiction of its members, remains a cornerstone of the UN system.

In the real world, of course, intervention rather than non-intervention is the rule. The history of international relations is a catalogue of ways and means employed by states to intervene in the internal affairs of other states — by armed force, intimidation, economic pressure, bribery, or numerous more subtle methods of persuasion. But precisely because reality is what it is, the principle of non-intervention is an essential element in the UN effort to create a more rational world order. It is one of those pretenses that are essential for civilized intercourse between governments. To abrogate Article 2:7 on the ground that it provides a shelter for tyrants would be tantamount to depriving honest citizens of the protection of the law because scoundrels also benefit from it.

Such is the power of the taboo against intervention in the internal affairs of a state that it has been broken in only one major case — that of the policy of apartheid practiced by the Republic of South Africa — and even this one case has had to be smuggled into the UN past Article 2:7 in the guise of a threat to international peace and security rather than as a systematic and massive denial of human rights. By thus reversing cause and effect the opponents of apartheid have made their case fit the priorities of the UN Charter which provides for sanctions against breaches of peace but not against violations of human rights.

The campaign against apartheid waged by and through the UN must be rated as the most successful of its kind in our time. It has made apartheid a household word as the symbol of supreme evil throughout the world. Whatever white people may say about it in private, any public mention of apartheid is automatically coupled with the equivalent of a curse. No other wrong in this world of so many wrongs elicits a comparable flood of universal condemnation and rejection.

The crime committed by the whites of the Republic of South Africa is said to be unique in that they have elevated racial segregation into a quasireligous doctrine and made it a centerpiece of their legal system. The same was, of course, done in Nazi Germany, but in the 1930s the taboo against intervention in the domestic affairs of a state was still inviolable. The contrast between then and now is revealing. The Western governments have been dragged along, reluctantly, first to admit that the issue of apartheid could be considered in the UN in spite of Article 2:7, then to accept the contention that it posed a threat to international peace and security, finally to go along with sanctions against the Republic of South Africa. While mandatory sanctions ordered by the Security Council only ban the sale of military equipment to South Africa, most Western countries, with the exception of Great Britain, have taken voluntarily measures to restrict economic relations as well.

The anti-apartheid campaign shows how powerful an instrument the UN can be for what is called "consciousness-raising" and forging a world-wide consensus on a particular issue. But it also reveals the limitations of UN action. The trumpet blasts of condemnation from the UN failed to bring down the wall around the white laager.

The Africans blame the major Western powers for not exerting maximum pressure on South Africa, and it is of course perfectly true that the Western nations have been inhibited by economic and strategic interests, and presumably also by unspoken solidarity with the white community. But the blacks also must share the blame, because in the 1960s and most of the 1970s, they believed the balance of power would evolve in their favor and force the white citadel to surrender in a relatively short time. The tone of the UN debates was set by the militants. To advocate peaceful change and a gradual social evolution was considered almost treasonable. The resolutions adopted by overwhelming majorities were in effect demands for the unconditional surrender of white power in South Africa.

It can never be proved whether or not a different approach would have been more effective, but I do believe an important opportunity was missed in 1966, when the United States for the first time joined the majority in the General Assembly in support of the independence of South West Africa, now Namibia, the former German colony which had been administered by the Republic of South Africa as a League of Nations mandate since the end of the first world war. A committee was set up to make recommendations as to how the independence of South West Africa could be implemented. Arthur Goldberg who was the architect of this change in United States policy persuaded William Rogers, a conservative Republican who had served as Attorney General in President Eisenhower's administration and later became President Nixon's Secretary of State, to represent the United

States on the committee and thus ensure bipartisan backing for whatever recommendations emerged. Goldberg's idea was that by opening a dialogue with South Africa the UN would get a foot in the door to a discussion on apartheid itself.

As chairman of the committee I worked hard to persuade the representatives of black Africa that it was in their interest to go along with this scheme, because only American pressure could induce the South African leaders to make concessions. This attempt at what later became known as "constructive engagement" was rejected by the radical Africans. They were egged on by the Soviet Union in the spirit of the global class struggle. The South West Africa committee failed to reach agreement on what to recommend to the General Assembly, and the notion of negotiations with South Africa was rejected by the majority. In 1967 the Assembly voted to create an independent state of Namibia. But for more than twenty years it remained a state existing on paper only. In the end, negotiations with South Africa were necessary to make Namibian independence a reality, but these negotiations were conducted outside the UN, under United States auspices.

By that time the context in which the negotiations were conducted had undergone a fundamental change. By supporting the opening of a dialogue with the South African government the Soviet Union removed the issue from the cold war agenda. The future of South Africa could no longer be presented as a stark choice between white and Western versus black and communist. Both sides were impelled by economic necessity toward reconciliation. Black Africa is a disaster area which desperately needs to put an end to the conflict; white South Africa must break out of its isolation to stop its economic decline.

Obviously, sanctions played a part in bringing about a change, though not quite in the way envisaged in the UN. As the world economy becomes more integrated, governments are less able to enforce the kind of trade embargoes or blockades prescribed in the UN Charter. Instead, the markets themselves punish a country that for one reason or another can no longer be considered a reliable or respectable trading partner. In the case of South Africa, the credit squeeze imposed by Western financial institutions has probably contributed more than all formal sanctions to persuading its leaders that the time has come to begin to dismantle the system of apartheid.

Now that South Africa has entered a period of internal dialogue, the UN faces a new kind of test. While it will still be necessary to maintain international pressure on the white leaders, the UN will have to move away from its all-or-nothing position and find ways to support and encourage black moderation. As elsewhere, South Africa's racial, ethnic and linguistic groups, having achieved their right to equality, will insist on their right to maintain their different identities: They will have to be protected against the tyranny of the majority.

The future political system of South Africa will have to be worked out by the South Africans themselves, but it will continue to be a matter of international concern: It will stay on the UN agenda for years to come. The long campaign against apartheid has developed its own liturgy and rituals. But other human rights issues are bound to receive increasing attention. This does not mean that human rights proceedings will be less politicized, more objective: in an intergovernmental organization everything is inevitably politicized. But the political context in which human rights issues are considered is changing. When the West was perceived to be on the defensive, proponents of collective values had the upper hand. The human rights debate was part of the East-West confrontation. Now the Soviet claim that in socialist societies the economic and social rights of citizens are better cared for than in the capitalist world has been discredited. Western opinion is also less inclined to turn a blind eye on violations of human rights in Third World countries. Post-colonial guilt is fading. With the West ascendant, Western liberal values gain greater respect. Even governments with a less than reputable record on human rights find it politically expedient to pay lipservice to democracy and individual freedom.

In these circumstances it may be possible to strengthen the UN machinery dealing with human rights. One step in that direction would be the creation of an office of a High Commissioner for Human Rights which was first proposed a quarter century ago, provided that a person of stature and integrity could be found for the job.

The United States has also proposed that the UN establish a special coordinator for electoral assistance, to be assisted by a UN electoral commission, to promote the spread of democratic government based on free elections. "Calls for democracy and human rights are being reborn everywhere," President George Bush declared in his speech to the General Assembly on October 1, 1990. According to statistics compiled by Freedom House of New York, liberal democracies now outnumber all other kinds of political systems. In 1990 the number of countries classified as free and the number of people living in them rose above 50 percent for the first time in 45 years.[4]

Such statistics, however, provide a somewhat shallow view of the global reality. In Latin America as well as in the former socialist states of Central and Eastern Europe, the fledgling democracies have inherited a crushing burden of external debt, industrial decay, and environmental degradation — not a promising ground for democratic values to take root in. In Africa, political elites may well have chosen democratic procedures less from profound conviction than from a desire to be on the winning side. All the newly established democracies expect to be amply awarded for their conversion. Expert advice on how to organize free elections will not be enough.

In multi-ethnic states the demand for free elections may be perceived as a threat to national unity. Such cases present the UN with a difficult dilemma. In a conflict between the principle of national self-determination and the integrity of existing state structures the UN, like all intergovernmental institutions, tilts in favor of the latter. For Nigeria against Biafra, for China against Tibet, for the Soviet Union against the Baltic republics, for Iraq against the Kurds.

Let us therefore not delude ourselves into believing, as Presidents Reagan and Bush have professed to do, that human rights, democracy, and free elections will now be lifted above all other issues in the UN. They have become more important in international politics, but their role in relations between governments is still marginal, not central.

Economic Development

If an honest poll could be taken among all the member governments of the UN as to their order of priorities, there can hardly be any doubt that a clear majority would put economic development at the top of the agenda. But if they then were asked to name the most important international instruments for promoting economic development, the UN would no longer make first place. Ten years ago, and certainly in earlier periods, the UN was believed to have a central role in international efforts to advance economic development in the Third World. It was the principal forum for the North-South dialogue. But the 1980s was a decade of disillusionment.

Before disillusionment there had to be illusions. The first was the American belief in the 1950s and early 1960s that a second Marshall Plan could launch the new independent states of the Third World on to a rising curve of economic development. Addressing the General Assembly in September 1961, President John F. Kennedy introduced his proposal for the first UN Development Decade: "Political sovereignty is but a mockery without the means of meeting poverty, illiteracy, and disease. Self-determination is but a slogan if the future holds no hope . . . ."

The UN Development Program (UNDP) was set up with Paul Hoffman, former administrator of the Marshall Plan, at its head. He was a true believer in the internationalist cause. But American enthusiasm for the UN Development Decade was also part of the great ideological contest between capitalism and communism. Both sides wooed the new states emerging from colonial rule with offers of economic assistance. After John Foster Dulles had lost to the Soviet Union, as it was said at the time, the privilege of building the Aswan dam for Nasser, Kennedy financed the construction of an equally huge dam in Upper Volta. The policy of a dam for a dam was pursued relentlessly throughout the Third World.

Western opinion was mesmerized by the colorful new actors on the world stage: Nehru, Nkrumah, Sekou Tour, Sukarno, Nasser, Nyerere, Kaunda . . . . The UN provided them with a platform to advance the claim that the peoples of the Third World were now entitled to receive their rightful share of the world's wealth which colonial rule had unjustly withheld from them. Their demand for justice, not charity, was received with sympathy. The UN was used to persuade the wealthy industrial countries that it was in their own interest to help the new states to develop their economies.

In hindsight, this first American-led phase in UN efforts to promote international cooperation for economic development appears to have been a mixture of arrogance and naiveté. It was arrogant to take it for granted that the Western model of economic development had universal validity. It was naive to believe in instant modernization. The ideological rivalry encouraged spectacular industrial projects at the expense of agriculture with disastrous consequences in many countries, particularly in Africa. It was naive, too, to idealize the politics of liberation and ignore the diversity of cultural backgrounds in the Third World. Criticism of the brutal methods employed by the great liberators to maintain their power was dismissed as neocolonialism. Democracy, it was widely held, was a luxury only the wealthy nations could afford. The leaders of poor and backward countries must be excused for using dictatorial means as the only way to economic development. Violations of human rights in such countries were growing pains that surely would pass as their economies improved. In the meantime tact was called for. Poor and backward was called "developing," wealthy and advanced "developed" and aid was called cooperation.

By the end of the first Development Decade the developing countries themselves had taken the lead in the UN. This marked the beginning of a new approach to the development issue. It was not enough for the developed countries to provide assistance; the structure of economic relations in the world also had to be changed before developing countries could have a genuine chance to improve their economic performance. A restructuring of the world economic system required planned policy actions on the part of both developed and developing states on a wide range of issues — commodity prices, trade in manufactured products, international shipping, the international monetary system, the transfer of technology, transnational corporations etc. Thus complex international conventions or other agreements had to be worked out on a global scale, and the UN, especially UNCTAD, became the principal forum for negotiations to this end.

The oil crisis of 1973 provided a powerful boost to the effort of the developing countries to restructure the world economy. The balance of power between North and South seemed to change dramatically, almost overnight. According to the Club of Rome, the industrial world was running out of resources and reaching the limits of growth. The nations that owned the larger part of the world's oil reserves and other primary commodities were therefore bound to gain the upper hand. As Kenneth Dadzie, the Director General of the UN, has written, the action taken by the oil producing countries in 1973 "lent credence to the possibility of fundamental change and to the aspiration that a world of economic equity and justice, as envisaged by the developing countries, might actually be created." Inspired by their new sense of "commodity power" the representatives of the developing countries put forward a detailed blueprint for what could be called a global Welfare State to be managed and regulated by the UN. It was adopted by the General Assembly in 1974 under the title of the New International Economic Order (NIEO).[5]

This was the second grand illusion of economic development. Although the governments of the industrial North paid lipservice to the principles of the NIEO, the consensus reached was a phony one. The North was not prepared to go along with the giant redistribution of incomes demanded by the South. The bargaining power of the developing countries proved to be short-lived. In the 1980s the glut in the oil market put an end to OPEC's political influence. Technological advances invalidated the predictions of the Club of Rome. The Western countries turned away from the welfare state and adopted free market policies, privatization and deregulation. As the role of government in national economies was reduced, the role of intergovernmental organizations in the world economy was reduced correspondingly. The idea of a UN-managed world economic system seems almost laughable today. A new international economic order has indeed taken shape, but it is a technology-driven, market-oriented, fiercely competitive order only marginally affected by individual government decisions.

With this structural change in the world economy, control over development policy has passed back to the developed countries. Collective bargaining between the "labor unions of the South and the management side of the North" is out. The developing countries are now told to put their own house in order by following the recipe of success — free market economies combined with democratic institutions — that has worked so well in North America, Western Europe, and Japan. Suddenly, the former indulgent attitude to dictatorships in developing countries has gone out of fashion. Now the conventional wisdom is that democracy is an indispensable prerequisite of economic progress.

But is this a new illusion? A quick look at the states of the Third World reveals that in many Asian countries where annual growth has reached double digits — South Korea, Singapore, Taiwan, Thailand, and Indonesia — have prospered under dictatorial leadership, while India, Malaysia, and Sri Lanka can be classified as democracies. In some cases success can be traced to the Confucian ethic, but Hindu India and Muslim Indonesia have also done relatively well. Every generalization breaks down when tested against reality.

In the debt-burdened Latin American countries transition from dictatorship to democracy has been accompanied by runaway inflation. In 1972, a much quoted editorial in the *Economist* asserted that two digit inflation would destroy democracy in Western Europe: how about four digit inflation in Argentina? Hardest hit has been Africa, the continent that has received more development aid per capita than any other — twenty dollars per person against seven dollars in Latin America and five in Asia. "Africa is a continent in dereliction and decay," Nigeria's former head of state Olusegul Obasanjo has said. Average per capita income has declined during the 1980s. Export value has fallen by nearly half, while capital inflows have shrunk. The debt burden has reached crisis proportions in more than half the Sub-Saharan countries. Since nearly half of Africa's current population is under age fifteen, a population surge will continue well into the twenty-first century. At current rates Africa's population will triple by 2025, in spite of the heavy toll taken by wars and disturbances as well as by AIDS and other diseases.

A UN Program of Action for African Economic Recovery and Development in 1986-90 was adopted at a special session of the General Assembly in 1986. But African leaders today acknowledge that external aid, though vitally necessary, cannot save the continent. According to Obasanjo, the cause of failure has been "our false political start." Only the Africans themselves can reform their political system.[6]

Such an admission represents a refreshing new candor. But it does not go so far as to question the very structure of post-colonial Africa. The borders of Africa's independent states were drawn by colonial administrators with little regard for ethnic or linguistic realities. In some cases people belonging to the same tribe and speaking the same language were divided; in others, people belonging to different tribes hostile to each other and unable to understand each other's languages were forced to live together. The colonial administrators kept order by stern measures; the world took little notice. But independence has not put an end to tribal conflicts. In fact, tribal loyalties tend to transcend loyalty to the state.

Burundi is a case in point. The two tribes inhabiting the country, the Hutus and the Tutsis, have been killing each other for centuries and have not been stopped by independence. A former US ambassador to Burundi, Thomas P. Melady, has proposed partition under UN auspices as the only way to prevent further slaughter.[7]   But any revisionist suggestion meets with fierce resistance from African governments that fear it might lead to the unravelling of the whole post-colonial structure and cause unimaginable chaos and endless strife. The bloody suppression of Biafra, the state of the Ibos of Nigeria, carried out with the support of virtually all of black Africa as well as of both Britain and the Soviet Union, was a grim warning to any one who might try his hand at revisionism. Thus black Africa remains imprisoned in its colonial past. But this is an unmentionable subject in the UN.

The stubborn fact of the 1980s, according to the president of the World Bank, is that "growth has been inadequate, poverty is still on the rise and the environment poorly protected. Unchanged, these realities would deny our children a peaceful decent and liveable world." In sub-Saharan Africa real income per head in 1988 was seventeen per cent less than in 1981, while the corresponding figure for Latin America and the Caribbean was around five percent or for the highly indebted countries over seven percent. By contrast, in East Asia the income per head rose by around sixty percent during the same period. Yet, owing to accumulated debt, the Third World countries are now paying back the First World more than fifty billion dollars more than the new money they receive from the West: the poor are subsidizing the rich. As the cost of interest payments in the 1980s has been over five times that of the 1970s, the indebted countries now have to divert an increasing proportion of national output from domestic consumption and investment to increase exports in order to earn enough foreign exchange, which is causing severe political and social consequences in many countries.

The policy of development assistance has also become subject to sharp criticism in the donor countries. That it is in the interest of the rich nations to help the poor is not disputed. Development assistance remains an integral part of the budget of every member of the OECD. While the UN target of 0.7 percent of GNP has been reached only by a few countries, the importance of official development assistance is illustrated by the fact that since the 1960s it has accounted consistently for over five percent of the GNP of some fifty developing countries. (It should be born in mind that seventy-five percent of this assistance is given by governments on a bilateral basis; about fifteen percent is channelled through the World Bank and other international financial institutions, and only six percent through the UN institutions.) But it is generally acknowledged today, by donors as well as recipients, that development assistance, amounting to forty-eight billion dollars a year, presents "a picture of incoherence and fragmentation, drawn by a multiplicity of donors, acting independently, with very different priorities, methods, and time frames, and in which the recipients themselves appear, perhaps by default, as background figures."[8]

Enter the Second World

A rethinking of development policy must be high on the UN agenda for the 1990s. It is a task made all the more urgent, and also more daunting, by two new factors: one is the dramatic change in East-West relations; the other, the growing importance of environmental issues both in the domestic politics of Western countries and in international relations.

What the change in East-West relations will mean in development policy in a material sense remains to be seen, but it is already clear that it will substantially affect the political context in which this issue will be considered in the UN and elsewhere. Until now, development policy has been a matter between the industrialized Western nations and the Third World. The Soviet Union and the other Socialist countries have disclaimed responsibility for helping the former colonies: let the imperialists pay for their crimes. The Soviet Union and its European allies have used their assistance programs to advance their ideological or strategic interests in the Third World. Such purposes are not unknown to Western policymakers, as can be seen from the fact that about two thirds of American development assistance is directed to the Middle East and Central America, the bulk of France's assistance to French speaking countries in Africa and the Pacific, and the greater part of Japan's aid to neighboring countries. The difference is, however, that the Western governments, unlike the Soviet bloc, also channel considerable amounts of assistance through the UN and other multi-lateral agencies in recognition of their general responsibility toward the South. Now President Gorbachev, too, speaks of the interdependence between developed and developing countries. He is prepared to put the "global problems of mankind" before ideological divisions and the international class struggle.

This is a momentous step. It promises to put an end to the ideological rivalry that has plagued development assistance for decades. This is what the leaders of the Third World have been praying for: The end of the Cold War was to release resources wasted on armaments for constructive efforts to help the poor nations to overcome their misery. But now this dream threatens to turn into a nightmare. The Soviet bloc nations have joined the breadline. The former communist countries, including the Soviet Union itself, now compete with the Third World for resources from the West. They are likely to push themselves to the head of the queue.

The West has a strong ideological interest in helping the former communist countries prove that democracy pays. European stability requires a joint effort to overcome the economic inequality between the two halves of the continent. Even more important, Western Europe is terrified of the prospect of large-scale migrations from East to West. It already faces formidable demographic pressures from North Africa and Turkey. In only ten years Turkey will have as many inhabitants as Italy and West Germany together, and by 2025 North Africa, including Egypt and Sudan, may have nearly as many inhabitants as will the twelve members of the European Community: 260 million against 306 million. By that same year, some fifty million Muslim immigrants from North Africa are expected to have settled in Western Europe to take up the jobs the aging European population no longer is able or willing to perform. An exodus from Central and Eastern Europe would add to the social strains already visible in West European societies and increase support for extremist parties exploiting racism or xenophobic sentiment. It makes sense to help the countries of Central and Eastern Europe improve conditions so that their people will stay at home. It is also in the Western interest to assist the former socialist countries to clean up their environment.

In spite of protestations to the contrary, aid to Central and Eastern Europe is bound to reduce the amount of Western resources available to the Third World. True, the amount of foreign assistance and government-backed credit authorized so far by Western countries for the Eastern half of Europe is quite small. By the end of 1990, the total amount of public foreign capital available was less than ten billion dollars: a modest sum compared to the debt burden that countries like Poland and Hungary currently carry. But then the outlook for development assistance is altogether bleak. A comparison between current aid programs for Central and Eastern Europe with the Marshall Plan is revealing. In 1989 prices the value of Marshall aid would be sixty-seven and a half billion dollars. Nothing even approaching this is imaginable in present circumstances.

The concept of a Marshall Plan is no longer applicable. Government-led projects on this scale are no longer feasible today when the role of government in the economy has been severely reduced. Where could comparable public funds come from today? The United States is still soaking up the financial capital surplus produced globally to finance its trade deficit. Of the two major surplus countries, Japan and Germany, the latter is now spending more than its surplus on rebuilding the eastern part of the country, while even the Japanese economy has been weakened by the recession that hit the developed countries in the beginning of 1990s.

The post-cold war "peace dividend" is shrinking fast before it has even had time to materialize. Hopes of sharp reductions in the military expenditures of the United States and other major Western countries were dashed by the Persian Gulf conflict, as well as by the resurgence of military influence in Soviet policy. Defense budgets will still be reduced, but probably much less than had been expected in the initial euphoria created by Gorbachev's reform policy. Whatever "peace dividend" will become available will primarily be used to reduce budget deficits and for social programs.

Given the state of political opinion in the United States and Western Europe, it would be unrealistic to count on any significant increase in official development assistance in the first years of the 1990s. As for the financial markets, the developing countries face tough terms. John Reed, the president of Citicorp, noted that of the 5 billion people living on earth "probably 800 million live within societies that are bankable and probably 4.2 billion within societies that in some very fundamental way are not bankable . . . We are forming this global economy that is very much a phenomenon of the northern hemisphere . . . Yet many of the problems we have on the globe, be it the global environment or health, are problems of the 4.2 billion, not the 800 million."[9]

In addition to swelling the ranks of applicants for aid, the end of the Cold War has had another important effect on development policy: Western governments now have no inhibitions against openly attaching political strings to development assistance. In the case of the former socialist countries of Central and Eastern Europe it has been taken for granted from the outset that aid will be given only so long as progress towards democracy and market economy continues. Now Third World countries face similar conditions. A document on the international development strategy for the 1990s adopted by consensus by the General Assembly in December 1990 points out that political freedom, respect for human rights, justice and equality, are "all essential and relevant to growth and development." The World Bank report on Africa states bluntly that African states must "improve governance" and make leaders "accountable to their peoples" in order to earn Western assistance.

How in practice improvements in the quality of governance or accountability will be determined remains to be seen, but the very fact that political conditions are now openly stated represents a profound change with far-reaching implications for international relations in general. Only a few years ago it would have been loudly condemned as inadmissible interference in the internal affairs of recipient countries. Today it is accepted as something "life itself", as the Russians might say, has imposed on governments.

One condition likely to figure more frequently in this context is insistence on a reduction of military expenditures.The World Bank has estimated that as much as one-third of the debt of some major Third World countries can be attributed to arms imports. Since the mid-1980s military expenditures in the Third World have declined (with the exception of Iraq and Iran), but it is still a staggering burden. Third World countries could create their own "peace dividend" by sharp reductions in military spending. The Independent Commission on Financial Flows (known as the Schmidt Commission after its chairman, former Chancellor Helmut Schmidt) suggested in its report issued in 1989 that as an inducement to disarmament in the Third World official development assistance should be increased to countries that spend less than two percent of their annual GNP on defense. This might be unfair to countries that have good reason to arm themselves against attacks from rapacious neighbors, but the idea is an interesting indication of the new trend in thinking on development issues.

The Ecological Challenge

Linking assistance to human rights and democracy or to arms control has fundamentally changed the context in which the issue of economic development is considered. Even more far-reaching consequences are likely to flow from the link between economic development and environmental protection.

The environmentalist agenda presents policymakers everywhere with a challenge that has no precedent in modern history. Like Marxism, it is based on what is claimed to be incontrovertible scientific truth, but not truth derived from the social sciences or history, but from the natural sciences which politicians find hard to argue against; unlike Marxism, it is not designed to improve the human condition, but to save nature from destruction by man and it is presented in the form of a series of categorical imperatives that must be obeyed.

As Marxism is losing its attraction, the radical idealism of young people gravitates towards the various green groups in Western societies. While the Green parties, in spite of their success in European elections in 1989, remain on the fringes of parliamentary power, their influence has grown far in excess of their voting strength, thanks largely to the media attention given to environmental issues. All political parties in the Western world are driven by the green demon.

Right and Left are divided on the need for government intervention to protect the environment, but there is also a deeper division emerging that cuts across the traditional Left-Right or East-West axis. It is between those who believe that the damage caused to the environment by technology can also be put right by technology and those who believe technology itself is the problem and therefore reject the goal of continued technology-driven economic growth as measured by GNP statistics. On this issue the UN is being divided along lines that are bound to shake up established alliances and groups.

A smooth compromise between the different philosophies was worked out by the World Commission on Environment and Development, chaired by Mrs. Gro Harlem Brundtland, the prime minister of Norway. In December 1983 the Commission had been asked by the UN General Assembly to produce "a global agenda for change." Its report, published in March 1987 under the heading "Our Common Future", forcefully made the point that environmental issues must not be treated in isolation from economic issues. The ecological crisis, the development crisis, the energy crisis, the population crisis: All are interrelated. Industry is the biggest polluter, but poverty, too, is a major cause of environmental degregation.

By presenting the environmental crisis as a potential threat to the security of nations the Brundtland Commission hopes to upgrade it on the scale of government priorities. Its final message is reassuring:

> "Humanity has the ability to make development sustainable — to ensure that it meets the needs of the present without compromising the ability of future generations to meet their own needs. . . . Technology and social organization can be both managed and improved to make way for a new era of economic growth. . . ."

Selling the concept of sustainable development to the world's nations is a task only the UN, as a global organization, can effectively undertake. In fact, however, the relevant agencies of the UN "tend to be independent, fragmented, working to relatively narrow mandates with closed decision processes." A more integrated approach is necessary — among states, as well as within the UN.[10]

In his annual report to the 1990 General Assembly session, Secretary-General Pérez de Cuellar stuck to the traditional hierarchy of issues, with security first and environment last, reflecting the order of priorities in the UN system. There is no high-level policy direction on environmental issues at UN headquarters in New York. The UN Environment Program (UNEP) has been tucked away in Nairobi, Kenya, a location chosen in the hope that the countries of the Third World would come to regard the problems of the environment as their own. But the practical effect has been that UNEP is short of funds and prestige, and is out of touch with the scientists and opinionmakers in the countries which count.

Now suddenly, an abundance of proposals to improve the capacity of the UN to deal with the environment has appeared. A wide range of ideas is under discussion: A permanent committee of the General Assembly, a new body comparable to the Security Council, the use of the Security Council itself for environmental issues, the elevation of UNEP to the status of a specialized agency, and so on. The Soviet Union has submitted a proposal for the UN to establish a center of emergency environmental assistance and to monitor the state of the earth environment from space. Similar suggestions on setting up a global watch and early warning system have been put forward by UNA.

Despite the doubts and ambiguities of the scientific analyses, a wide political consensus is emerging on the need for global action to counteract the "greenhouse effect" of a rise in average world temperature. The potentially grave consequences of global warming have been well publicized, though it is by no means the only environmental problem that needs urgent attention. The difference is that most other environmental problems can effectively be tackled locally or regionally; the warming of the world climate must be dealt with globally. It effects every nation, and effective counter-measures depend on world-wide cooperation.

A comprehensive review of environmental problems will be carried out at the UN Conference on Environment and Development to be held in Brazil in 1992. The goal is to work out guidelines, probably in the form of an international convention, for what could be called "good climatic behavior". It will be complemented with specific protocols, like the Montreal Protocol on Ozone Depletion which came into force in 1989. In this way a legal framework for controlling and regulating activities affecting the world climate will be established.

"Good climatic behavior" is a deceptively innocuous phrase. In fact it calls for fundamental changes in our industrial civilization. The greenhouse effect is caused primarily by the process of industrialization — in particular by the burning of fossil fuels. But it is also a consequence of changes in land use, in particular deforestation, in the poorer parts of the world where the relentless growth of population generates increasing pressure on the natural environment. Here is the vital — and fatal — link between environment, economic development, energy and population.

The ability of the world's political system to deal with environmental interdependence is coming under increasing strain. Global treaties regulating the behavior of states — like the law of the sea treaty, for instance — take about 15 years to negotiate and enter into force, and several more years for changes in behavior to actually occur. Normally, such treaties, once completed, are considered final and permanent. Ecologists insist that changes in climatic behavior must be achieved more quickly: Thomas Lovejoy, the prominent biologist, for example, said he was utterly convinced that "most of the great environmental struggles will be either won or lost in the 1990s and by the next century it will be too late." The traditional static treaty model must give way to a more fluid that allows for adjustments in response to new scientific knowledge. A new system will also have to take into account the power of the market. As governments have less control over economic activities, the private sector must be involved, not as an adversary but as a partner. International regimes that regulate the environmental conduct of states face problems of monitoring and enforcing. It has been suggested, by the Soviet government among others, that the Security Council might be assigned a role as enforcer. The concept of international security would therefore be redefined to include environmental issues. Since pollution in one country can threaten the vital interests of its neighbors, it should be considered the equivalent of military aggression and treated accordingly: Let the Five Policemen do their job!

There is, however, a fundamental flaw in this reasoning. The military power of the five permanent members of the Security Council in no way qualifies them to run a global environmental policy. China and the Soviet Union are among the world's worst polluters, nor are the other three models of environmental rectitude. "Ecological aggression" cannot be dealt with by military means. Other methods more in tune with present-day world conditions will have to be devised to ensure compliance with environmental treaties. This will present "environmental diplomacy" with a complex task. A Climate Treaty is obviously vulnerable to cheating. To prevent it both a stick and a carrot will be needed. The countries that will lose least in economic growth by limiting emissions of greenhouse gases will have to compensate those that lose most, while some type of trade sanctions will have to be used to stop free riders.

Reforming the UN System

A new, more integrated approach to these complex issues is urgently required, as the Brundtland Commission has pointed out. It is not enough to strengthen and upgrade existing UN units dealing specifically with the environment. It will be necessary to review the entire range of UN activities in the economic and social field with a view to reshaping the organization for the tasks it faces in the 1990s. The reviews carried out so far have not gone to the heart of the matter. They have suggested ways in which the present organization could be made to function more efficiently, but what is needed now is a reappraisal of the basic assumptions underlying the present organization.

Today, parts of the UN that deal with economic and social issues reflect the effort of the developing countries to create the New International Economic Order. While the Third World lacked the political and economic strength to carry through a restructuring of the world economy, it did have the voting power to restructure the UN. The organization was refitted to serve as the executive and administrative center of the NIEO. Between 1974 and 1980 more than two dozen new agencies were created in the UN system, almost all of them, as stated in their founding resolutions, established to implement the programs of the NIEO. In the same period, more than a dozen new special funds were established to finance the programs of the new order. The UN Secretariat was similarly reorganized for the same purpose.

The NIEO never materialized, but its supporting institutions remain.[11] The UN system resembles an army equipped and deployed to fight an enemy that has vanished. As a result, the governments of the wealthy North have turned their back on it, while the South is disillusioned and fragmented. The many UN bodies dealing with economic issues — the Second Committee of the General Assembly, the Economic and Social Council, UNCTAD, UNIDO — grind away year after year on their massive agendas producing resolutions that governments take little notice of and the media none at all.

A report of a study group of the World Institute for Development Economics Research (WIDER), published in May 1989, goes so far as to suggest the creation of a new international body — a World Economic Council — to carry out a reform of existing global multilateral institutions and, more generally, supervise and coordinate "global macroeconomic policy." The report points out that key decisions on the debt problem, the setting of international exchange rates and other issues affecting the world economy are taken within a limited group of developed countries. This inner core consists of the so-called G-5 and the G-7 countries. (Britain, France, Germany, Japan, and the United States are the five, with Canada and Italy added to make seven.) This leaves the Third World out in the cold. The G-7 have admitted representatives of Third World countries to their summit only once, at Cancun, Mexico, in 1981.

The WIDER study group suggests that the smaller industrial countries and the developing countries — "the Non-Five" — join forces and delegate authority to a representative group which would participate in the world summit. The report presents an elaborate scheme for a voting system for the countries of the Non-Five, "based upon three objective criteria reflecting their economic and political weight in the world — GNP, trade, and population."[12]

This ingenuous scheme is not likely to be put into effect in the foreseeable future. It is just not possible to stop allied or like-minded governments from meeting amongst themselves in order to coordinate their policies. The G-7 may be persuaded to meet with representatives of the developing countries from time to time, but only in addition to, and not in place of, their own summits. Another objection is that the group of Non-Five is in reality a non-group of countries with widely diverse economic interests. No voting system, however objective, is likely to persuade governments to delegate to others the authority to make decisions on vital issues. Such a delegation of authority has not been possible within the UN: Why should it be possible outside of it?

The report of the WIDER study group, which included a number of distinguished and experienced international public servants, is nevertheless a significant contribution to the debate on the state of the existing system of multilateral economic cooperation. Its institutions were constructed at the end of the second world war, at a time when the international economic system consisted of distinct national economies with governments in control of external economic transactions. At the time the United States accounted for forty percent of the world's combined GNP; in Western Europe a Keynesian consensus on the role of the state in the economy was predominant; the Soviet Union and the other socialist countries had withdrawn into isolation; and what today is called the Third World was still largely under colonial rule. None of these conditions prevails today. Economic power is more widely dispersed; the internationalization of capital movements has sharply curtailed the ability of governments to control economic developments; the countries of the Third World account for a growing part of the global GNP. In addition, concern for the environment — surprisingly not mentioned in the WIDER report — has introduced a new element into the making of "global macroeconomic policy." The system of 1945 is in a state of decay. But while the need for reform is obvious, the political will to undertake it is still lacking. Unlike 1945 when the United States was strong enough to create an economic system in accordance with its own vision of the postwar world, today a restructuring of the multilateral institutions would require a concerted effort by all the major powers. For the time being, they seem to be content to do things through ad hoc arrangements.

Before proposing to set up yet another new international institution the reformers ought to consider what can be done to make better use of the existing ones. A number of proposals to revitalize the economic and social functions of the UN are on the table. The Secretary-General has suggested that ECOSOC, a body of fifty-four member states, be transformed into a council of ministers, backed up by a policy-planning staff for development at UN headquarters. Another proposal is to cut down the size of ECOSOC to a maximum of twenty-seven members and mandate it to give priority to urgent economic and social issues that are not within the jurisdiction of the Security Council. Finally, UNA has come up with the idea of creating a small senior ministerial board within ECOSOC, while expanding ECOSOC itself to include all member states and eliminating the second and third committees of the General Assembly in order to reduce duplication.[13]

The purpose of each of these proposals is to get the important states to return to the UN for discussions on economic and social issues. The trouble is that this sort of institutional reform is like designing a new product in the hope that its appearance on the market will create demand for it. My own experiences of a similar attempt make me skeptical of the possibilities of success. In 1970, when Finland was a member of the Security Council, I proposed that the Council begin to hold regular meetings at which each member state would be represented by its foreign minister. The idea was by no means original. The Charter stipulates, in Article 27, that "the Security Council shall hold periodic meetings at which each of its members may, if it so desires, be represented by a member of the government or by some other specially designated representative." Each Secretary-General had tried to persuade the major powers to hold such meetings. In fact, not one single periodic meeting had ever been held. In 1970 conditions seemed right to make a new attempt. East-West detente had fostered cooperation between the major powers in the UN. Regular ministerial meetings, I argued, would make it possible for the Security Council to play a constructive part in preventing conflicts in stead of only reacting to violent events. The authority of the UN would be enhanced. The foreign ministers of the major powers would no longer have to spend so much time on discussing when and where to meet, or worry about inflated public expectations that precede every summit. The routine of periodic meetings of the Security Council would enable them to maintain regular contact and would provide the Secretary- General with a valuable platform.

The non-permanent members of the Security Council were enthusiastic about my proposal. The permanent members brooded over it. After about six months they finally agreed, probably because no one could think of a good argument against it. The first ever periodic meeting was held on October 21, 1970, with the foreign ministers of all five permanent members present. After a discussion behind closed doors, they issued a statement unanimously endorsing periodic meetings as a means for strengthening the capacity of the UN to maintain international peace and security. The Council seemed ready to making periodic meetings truly periodic. But almost ten years passed without another one. The second was held in 1979, and none since then.

The lesson for ECOSOC is obvious: you can take a horse to the water but you cannot make it drink. The ministers may attend once, but will they come a second time? ECOSOC has lost its credibility as a forum for dealing with important economic issues and now will have to work its way back into the confidence of powers through a new integrated approach to the many interrelated economic, social and environmental problems of our time.

In theory, the Secretary-General commands unique resources as chairman of the Administrative Committee on Coordination (ACC) which brings together the executive heads of the entire galaxy of special agencies within the UN system. Potentially this group could act as a kind of super-cabinet with an agenda of global issues. In practice, however, each agency is a separate, sovereign international body with its own charter, membership, budget, and assembly of national representatives. The ACC meets only two or three times a year and its coordinating function is largely symbolic.

A genuine integrated approach cannot be achieved on the UN level before the governments of member states themselves adopt it on a national level. As long as every department fiercely defends its own turf within national cabinets the specialized agencies continue to assert their autonomy against the Secretary-General of the UN. In New York, delegations of member governments urge the Secretary-General to achieve better overall coordination, but the delegations of the same governments in the assemblies of the various specialized agencies support a policy that runs counter to the demands of coordination. Even the UN itself, the parent body as it were, is fragmented by the large number of semi-autonomous units set up to deal with a great variety of tasks. Clearly, some deconstruction is called for before a reconstruction of the UN system can be carried out. But this is bound to meet with strong political and bureaucratic resistance.

While the global economic and social issues are being discussed in the various UN bodies on a high level of generalization, operative control over international development policy has been taken over by the International Monetary Fund and the World Bank. As President George Bush pointed out, "in a world where ideology no longer confronts and big power blocs no longer divide, the Bank and the Fund have become paradigms of international cooperation." As these institutions cease to be purely Western and become universal in membership, a more rational division of labor is emerging within the UN system. Many representatives of developing countries resist this, for understandable reasons: the UN is like a parliamentary body in which each member has one vote, while the Fund and the Bank are like corporations in which each member holds a certain number of shares. In addition, the Fund is widely resented in developing countries as a stern custodian of financial rectitude. In the words of former President Julius Nyerere of Tanzania, the Fund makes errant countries "starve their children to pay their debts" — except, of course, the biggest sinner of all, the United States. But the dismal experiences of the 1970s revealed the futility of any attempt to use the voting power of the developing countries in the UN to tax the rich. It is in the interest of the developing countries themselves to go where the money is and concentrate their efforts on the Fund and the Bank.

There are additional ways in which the developing countries could make their voice heard in the councils of the rich. One is to insist on closer coordination between the UN and the specialized agencies, including the Fund and the Bank. Another — a shortcut — is for the Secretary-General to follow in Gorbachev's footsteps and solicit an invitation to the next summit meeting of the G-7. The president of the Commission of the European Community has already been admitted. Why not also the Secretary-General of the UN as spokesman for the 4.2 billion people who live in the "unbankable" parts of the world?

V

LEADERSHIP

Virtually every discussion I have had with members of the UN community about the future prospects of the Organization has ended with a prayer for leadership. This must come from the governments of the major powers, particularly the United States, and influential groups of medium and smaller states, like the Nordic countries. But leadership must also come from the appointed officials of the Organization — above all from the Secretary-General.

Everyone pays tribute to the incumbent, Javier Pérez de Cuellar, for his integrity and diplomatic skills, but he will be seventy-one at the conclusion of his second five-year term at the end of 1991 and has stated that he will not be available for a third period. So the search for a new Secretary-General is on. Expectations are mounting. To meet all of them he or she will have to be a great communicator like Ronald Reagan, a bold reformer like Mikhail Gorbachev, a master diplomat like Henry Kissinger, a super-manager like Lee Iacocca. But if such a person can be found, will the governments of the major powers agree to accept him? And will he himself be willing to be chained to that proverbial rack of torture, the Procrustean bed, alternately stretched beyond reason by the demands of "We the peoples" in whose name the UN Charter has been written, and cruelly cut down to size by the realities of power?

The contradiction between expectations and constraints was built into the office of the Secretary-General at its inception. At the San Francisco Conference in 1945, the Big Five still believed they would jointly run the world organization; they needed an office manager, not a policymaker. Accordingly, the Soviet foreign minister proposed that the Secretary-General and four Deputy Secretaries-General be nationals of the five major powers, each elected for a two-year term. That way,

155

within a decade, a national of each of the Big Five could serve as Secretary-General. But the smaller nations strongly objected to such blatant domination by the five veto powers, and the British, drawing on their own political tradition, introduced the concept of an independent international civil service. As often happens in multilateral negotiations, the document that finally emerged perpetuates rather than resolves the differences. Both concepts were written into the Charter, with the result that the chapter on the Secretary-General is like a photograph with double exposure. In accordance with the wishes of the smaller nations, the Secretary-General shall be appointed by the General Assembly, but first he must receive "the recommendation of the Security Council", which means that each of the five veto powers can blackball any candidate.

Further, the Secretary-General is described as "the chief administrative officer" who shall perform such functions as are entrusted to him by the principal organs, but he is also granted the right to take political initiatives by virtue of Article 99, which permits him to "bring to the attention of the Security Council any matter which in his opinion may threaten the maintenance of international peace and security." Finally, the high ideals of an independent international civil service were written into the Charter in Article 100, which states that "the Secretary-General and the staff shall not seek or receive instructions from any government . . ." Yet the Big Five immediately agreed to divide between their own nationals the posts of principal advisers to the Secretary-General.

At San Francisco, the misgivings of the smaller nations were forcefully expressed by the delegate of the Netherlands, who argued that subjecting the choice of the Secretary-General to the veto would compel the permanent members to seek a compromise candidate which represent the "lowest common denominator." He feared the Secretary-General would have to show "more talent for tact toward the major powers than common sense and integrity." But once the eagles had spoken, the twittering of the smaller birds was to no avail.[1]

Looking back over the past four decades it must be admitted that, with the exception of Dag Hammarskjöld during his second term in 1956–61, none of the Secretaries-General has been able to play a strong role of political leadership, nor has any excelled as an administrator. While the political influence of the Secretary-General has been severely circumscribed by the permanent members of the Security Council, his administrative authority has been whittled away by the Third World majority in the General Assembly.

If the system tends to result in the appointment of a lowest common denominator, how did Dag Hammarskjöld get elected? The answer is a tale full of ironies.

In spring of 1954, the office of the Secretary-General had been virtually paralyzed for more than two years. The choice of the Norwegian labor politician Trygve Lie as the first Secretary-General seemed a reasonable compromise between the leading members of the Grand Alliance. His country had a tradition of neutrality and of international humanitarian service. As a social-democrat he was thought, in the misguided optimism of the time, to represent a middle way between capitalism and communism. But the Cold War put an end to the spirit of compromise. The North Korean invasion of the South Korea in 1950 was a fatal turning point for the first Secretary-General. His support of the Security Council's decision to endorse the U.S. action to defend South Korea led to a rupture of his relations with the Soviet Union. From then on the Soviet delegation refused to have anything to do with him.

It is hard to see how he could have avoided losing the confidence of one or the other of the two superpowers. Less defensible was his craven submission to the insistence of the United States to investigate the loyalty of American citizens employed by the UN secretariat — their loyalty to the United States rather than to the UN. Those found wanting were dismissed forthwith: so much for the noble principles of Article 100 of the Charter. As a result, Trygve Lie lost the confidence of his own staff. He also managed to irritate the Western governments by his pretensions to act like the "foreign minister of the world". But so long as the Korean war went on there was no hope of reaching agreement on a successor.

The post-Stalin phase in the Soviet Union finally opened the way to armistice negotiations in Korea and a search for a new Secretary General. Trygve Lie resigned in November 1952, but it took until March 1953 for the Security Council to name a successor. After canvassing a long list of prominent persons, none of whom found favor with the Soviets, the Council produced a surprise name acceptable to all: Dag Hammarskjöld. Dag who? was the reaction of most people. He was known only in the narrow circle of professional diplomats who had been impressed by his ability as head of the Swedish delegation at the Marshall Plan conference in Paris. The son of a former prime minister, Dag Hammarskjöld was a member of the ruling class of Sweden, that is, non-political civil servants, the mandarins who have run the country for centuries and made it such a well-functioning, orderly, and boring society. A neutral bureaucrat from neutral Sweden seemed just the right man to deal with the administrative mess left by Trygve Lie. Hammarskjöld was known as an aloof intellectual with esoteric cultural interests who surely would cause the major powers no trouble. Initially, his own aspirations were also modest. His sense of mission developed only gradually. Like an explorer he set out to find a new world. "Working at the edge of the development of human society is to work on the brink of the unknown," he once said.[2]

So powerful was the impact of Hammarskjöld's performance as Secretary-General that his ghost has hovered in the background at the election of each of his successors. Every candidate has been tested by the Soviets for possible infection by the Hammarskjöld-virus: A positive reaction has meant disqualification. In fact none of his successors has ventured to explore the edge of the unknown in world politics. U Thant did defy the government of one of the two superpowers by his criticism of United States policy on Vietnam. But in doing so he was voicing the opinion of his constituency, the *non-aligned group,* and he knew he could do this with impunity because the state of opinion in the United States itself protected him against retaliation by Washington. By the end of U Thant's second term in 1971, the issue of the independence of the Secretary-General in relation to the permanent members of the Security Council was no longer at the center of the debate about his successor. The two superpowers had reached an unspoken agreement to prevent the election of a Third World candidate. This meant that the choice would have to be made from the candidates of the three European neutral countries, each of whom could be relied upon to work within the framework of the American-Soviet détente.

A laconic comment published in Pravda on the eve of the election of the Secretary-General in December 1971 told the whole story. All it said was that there were three candidates to succeed U Thant: Kurt Waldheim of Austria, Gunnar Jarring of Sweden, and Max Jakobson of Finland. These few lines managed to convey two messages. One was the omission of the names of the several Third World candidates who were publicly contending for the post; the other was that the order in which the three names were listed, since it was not alphabetical, revealed Moscow's preferences.

The events leading up to the final decision just before Christmas 1971 provided, in the words of Brian Urquhart, "a sad impression of lack of top-level governmental interest, inadequate high-level consultation, opportunism, gossip, rumor, intrigue, and a complete absence of record-checking."[3]

In the voting, Jarring was vetoed by the United States, Britain and China, Waldheim by Britain and China, and I was vetoed by the Soviet Union. From this Moscow was able to infer that the United States, at the time represented by George Bush, had no objection to Waldheim, although it had placed me first in its own order of preferences. In this situation the Soviet, as usual, proved to be master of tacticians. They succeeded in presenting the choice as being one between Waldheim or a deadlock that would paralyze the Organization. Subsequently, Britain and then China withdrew their veto, while the Soviets maintained theirs against me, and so Waldheim was finally elected.

Both superpowers practiced what is called damage limitation. Washington, I imagine, was relieved to learn that the Soviet government was prepared to accept the former foreign minister of Austria, a man who could cause no problems for the United States. In any event, in December 1971 Nixon and Kissinger were preoccupied with preparations for the all-important Moscow summit. They were not inclined to pick a quarrel with the Soviets over a secondary issue.

Everyone in the UN knew at the time that Waldheim had served in the German army during the second world war as had all able-bodied Austrian men of his age. No one brought this up in the discussions on the qualifications of the various candidates. Waldheim's war record acquired a sinister connotation only after the publication in 1984 of his autobiography which failed to mention his participation as a junior staff officer in the German campaign in the Balkans. It raised questions that still remain without answer: Was the Soviet government so keen on promoting Waldheim's candidacy because it knew something about his past that could be used to blackmail him? Did the United States government have a similar motive for supporting him? I for one do not believe in such conspiracy theories. Neither the Soviets nor the Americans needed to resort to blackmail to ensure his pliancy. According to Brian Urquhart, who was Waldheim's principal political adviser for ten years, "Waldheim was an energetic, ambitious mediocrity." George Bush found him a congenial companion.

Article 99

In his first public statement as Secretary-General, Waldheim emphasized that "in this position one has to know the limits." These words have often been quoted as evidence of his submissiveness, but at that time any one would have had to know the limits. But instead of trying to extend them, Waldheim narrowed them even further by his compulsive campaigning for reelection. In this he was successful. In 1976 he was reappointed for a second five-year term, and in 1981 the two superpowers were prepared to support him for a third term. But this time the Chinese put their foot down. They had shown their disapproval of Waldheim in 1971 and again in 1976 by using their veto in a couple of rounds of voting before bowing to the will of the superpowers. In 1981, they refused to give in, insisting on the election of a candidate from the Third World. The United States, with the silent backing of the Soviet Union, was determined to prevent the election of a militant African candidate. A subtle compromise was found in the person of Javier Pérez de Cuellar: as a Peruvian he represents a Third World country, but as a professional diplomat he is in the European tradition — the opposite of a militant.

The new Secretary-General was quick to distance himself from his predecessor by declaring that he would serve one term only. The idea of limiting the Secretary-General to one term — of six or seven years instead of the present five — without the right to reelection has received a great deal of support within the UN. No doubt it would be a way to prevent a future Waldheim from yielding to temptation, but it would have no relevance to getting a strong person elected. Actually,

Pérez de Cuellar himself agreed to a second term 1986, having first obtained from the US government promises of action to relieve the Organization's financial crisis.

More to the point is to examine the limits Waldheim referred to: What could be done to strengthen the capacity of the Secretary-General to play an independent political role? The Charter as it stands is good enough. Article 99, though vague, gives him wide authority, not only to react to an actual crisis, but also to anticipate potential conflicts and propose preventive action. The astonishing fact is, however, that Article 99 has been explicitly invoked only once during the forty-five years of the UN's existence. This was in May 1960, when Dag Hammarskjöld used it to call the Security Council into session over the Congo crisis. Each of his successors has once used the language of Article 99, without invoking it explicitly, to convene the Security Council: U Thant during the India-Pakistan war in 1971, Waldheim during the Iranian hostage crisis in 1979, Pérez de Cuellar with reference to Lebanon in 1989.

Both U Thant and Pérez de Cuellar have taken great pains to justify their record on this point. According to U Thant, the "quiet method of forestalling conflict" is preferable to creating a public confrontation in the Security Council: "Nothing could be more divisive and useless than for the Secretary-General to bring a situation publicly to the Security Council when there is no practical possibility of the Council's agreeing on effective or useful action."[4] Pérez de Cuellar has offered a more elaborate analysis. Before invoking Article 99, he has written, "The Secretary-General has to consider carefully how his initiative will fare, given the agreement or lack thereof among the permanent members and also the positions of the non-permanent members. A situation may in certain cases be aggravated and not eased if the Secretary-General draws attention, under Article 99, and the Security Council then does nothing. Situations that threaten the peace are usually highly complicated and require a flexible and finely tuned response from the Secretary-General. . . . Two situations with equally dangerous potential may have to be dealt with in two different ways, depending on how far they can be insulated from great power rivalries, how far the parties are susceptible to moral suasion, and, in some cases, whether one or both of them is reluctant to face exposure in the Security Council. . . ." Over the years, he has pointed out, the practice has grown for the Secretary-General himself to help to moderate conflicts or negotiate solutions, without formal invocation of Article 99.[5]

Quiet diplomacy practiced by successive Secretaries-General has indeed been a valuable service to the international community. There is an impressive list of cases in which the Secretary-General has used his "good offices" to mediate between states, either at the request of a UN organ or in response to the wishes of the parties to a dispute. In some instances the Secretary-General has even intervened in a crisis entirely on his own authority. The diplomatic activities of the Secretary-General have ranged widely over the globe, from Cyprus, Afghanistan and the Persian Gulf to Western Sahara and even the Rainbow Warrior dispute between New Zealand and France, to mention only recent examples. The "good offices" function of the Secretary-General has never received the public recognition it deserves, partly because by its nature, The ability to defuse a crisis is to deprive it of news value.

Important as the "good offices" function is, it is nevertheless difficult to accept that there has not been one single instance in the past thirty years when the explicit use of Article 99 could have been justified. A preference for quiet diplomacy is of course understandable, if the alternative is to court the displeasure of a major government, but it is hardly credible that it is the only possible response to every crisis. The atrophy of Article 99 reveals, that the "limits" Waldheim talked about have been partly self-imposed.

Many conflicts have been brought to the Security Council by the parties themselves, but in a number of cases only an initiative by the Secretary-General could have activated the Council. The situation in the Middle East in May 1967 and the mounting tension between Iran and Iraq in the summer of 1980 are obvious examples. True, in each case, one or both of the parties to the conflict was "reluctant to face exposure in the Security Council", as Pérez de Cuellar put it. But the power of exposure is the only power the Secretary-General has. "The Secretary-General must always be prepared to take an initiative," U Thant has written, "no matter what the consequences to his office or to him personally may be, if he sincerely believes that it might mean the difference between peace and war. In such a situation, the personal prestige of the Secretary-General — and even the position of his office — must be considered to be expendable."[6] Yet, in May 1967, U Thant did not consider the situation dangerous enough to risk his own position.

The power to alert the world to the dangerous implications of a crisis and publicly confront the governments of the major powers with their duty to maintain peace is a heavy weapon in the hands of the Secretary-General. It can only be used in an extremely critical situation. But if the situation was not critical enough in 1967 or 1980, how critical must it be for the Secretary-General to resort to Article 99? It is rapidly becoming the diplomatic equivalent of the nuclear bomb — unusable.

There is another way of approaching Article 99. The Secretary-General could take the drama out of it by making much more active use of his right to draw the attention of the Security Council to matters which in his opinion may threaten the maintenance of international peace and security. According to Pérez de Cuellar, one reason why this has not been possible is the lack of independent sources of information available to the Secretary-General. To remedy this, he has set up an Office for Research and Collection of Information. This "watch" unit processes unclassified information from the media and from UN information centers around the world, maintains data files, coordinates the analytic work done in various secretariat departments, takes advantage of material from outside institutions and provides directly to the Secretary-General information and advice relevant to conflict prevention. The office has at present modest resources, but is planning to improve its communications system in order to alert the Secretary-General, and through him the Security Council, to potential crises in different parts of the world.

Even so, the means available to the Secretary-General of obtaining up-to-date information are primitive by comparison with those at the disposal of most governments. The Secretariat is not a sovereign entity with a world-wide network of embassies; as a servant of the member states, it cannot set up an intelligence service to find out what its masters are up to. In areas where a UN peacekeeping operation is in place the Secretary-General receives reports directly from his own representatives, but otherwise he must rely on published information or whatever representatives of governments may pass on to him.

Pérez de Cuellar has appealed to member states to give him the tools he needs to practice preventive diplomacy. "It is far more difficult to stop hostilities after their outbreak," he noted, "than to restrain governments from heading towards the point of no return." He argues for a "war preventing center" at the UN, capable of obtaining "timely, accurate, and unbiased information", in order to determine whether and when an issue needs to be brought to the attention of the Security Council under Article 99. Incipient conflicts must be kept under "a global watch". In order to monitor potential conflict situations "from a clearly impartial standpoint" the Secretariat should be receiving information from space-based and other technical surveillance systems. All this, the Secretary-General points out, "implies a conscious policy decision on the part of member states to strengthen and use the mediatory capacity of the Organization."

The concept of a war preventing center received the enthusiastic support of the Soviet government which not only endorsed the Secretary General's ideas about defusing potential conflicts between states, but also recommended "the prevention and removal of tension created by internal socio-economic and other causes" and the establishment under UN auspices of an international monitoring and control system and an international survey satellite agency to verify observance of disarmament agreements. The Soviets have also suggested the use of UN services to provide early warning of potential economic crises, environmental emergencies and natural and industrial disasters.

Pérez de Cuellar and the Soviet representatives, in spite of the ideological gulf between them, are both children of the enlightenment and share the belief that if only objective information, the unvarnished truth, the plain facts can be obtained, men will draw the correct conclusions and make the right decisions. But this faith in the power of the facts to produce rational action is not supported by historical experience. The flood of information, secret as well as public, pouring into the major capitals twenty-four hours a day from all parts of the world has not prevented governments from committing one ghastly blunder after another. The March of Folly, described by Barbara Tuchman as "the pursuit of policy contrary to the self-interest of the state involved", has not come to a halt in the Information Age. Time and again in recent decades, political leaders have ignored or misinterpreted facts and rejected sound advice, instead of taking action, which has led to disastrous results for their own country as well as for others.[7]

The UN Secretary-General did not need any special information in May 1967 to understand that war between Israel and the Arab states was imminent. Every intelligent reader of the *New York Times* was aware of the danger. In the summer of 1980, the mounting tension between Iran and Iraq was fully reported in the media. The agony of Lebanon has been witnessed by television viewers all over the world. In none of these cases has the UN been handicapped by any lack of information. Action has been prevented by a lack of political will.

An Independent Secretariat?

The vision of a UN war prevention center receiving "unbiased reports" by satellite from the world's trouble spots belongs to science fiction. It is hardly likely the UN scanners could uncover a crisis the media missed. What the Secretary-General does need is a first-rate team of independent analysts to help him evaluate what is going on in the world and draw the right conclusions for possible action.

The problem is conceptual, not technical. It is about the character of the Secretariat. The Charter is unusually clear on this point. Article 100 forbids any improper dealings between members of the Secretariat and national governments; Article 101 states that "the paramount consideration in the employment of the staff . . . shall be the necessity of securing the highest standard of efficiency, competence, and integrity." Only as an afterthought it adds that "due regard shall be paid to the importance of the grouping of the staff on as wide a geographical basis as possible." Accordingly, the Secretariat ought to be an independent international service representing the common interest of the membership as a whole and should be able to take its own initiatives on the basis of a detached interpretation of that interest. In reality, however, the governments of member states, while paying lipservice to Article 100, tend to view the Secretariat as an extension of the system of nation states. As a result, the Secretariat suffers from a chronic conflict between its internationalist mandate and its baser nationalist instincts.

I know from my own experience that there are many members of the Secretariat who live up to the principles of Article 100. But many others who hardly bother to conceal their contempt for them. It would be naive to believe that only officials from the Soviet bloc or other totalitarian states violate the principles of Article 100. Many others do it too, though less blatantly.

The main fault lies with the governments of the member states rather than with the individuals. There is no government too high-minded to refrain from lobbying for jobs for its own nationals. Not only have the major powers divided the principal posts among themselves, but a large number of lesser offices are also considered to belong by right to citizens of individual states or groups of states. A person who has been seconded by his government to serve a limited period of time in the UN Secretariat may in fact act in an impartial manner, but the perception is otherwise. Some Western officials receive a supplementary salary from home, and some nationals of the socialist states have part of their UN pay docked by their governments. Neither system conforms with the spirit of Article 100.

None of the Secretaries-General has seriously resisted pressures from the governments of member states on recruitment of staff. It is now commonplace to say that the entire UN system has become a bloated bureaucracy riddled with incompetent political appointees. Is it not what each of us tends to say about the civil service in his own country? The defects of bureaucracy inevitably are multiplied in an intergovernmental organization with 165 member states, very few of which share the British tradition of a non-political civil service. Standards in the Secretariat cannot possibly reach the level of the civil service in the wealthy countries of the world, but they are probably higher than the average across the diverse membership.

Statistics show, that contrary to popular belief executive posts in the UN system are not held predominantly by nationals of Third World countries. Western European and North American nationals have occupied the majority of such posts at all times since 1946: as much as seventy-nine percent in the first period before decolonization and sixty-two percent after 1970. In the major UN organizations the share of West Europeans and North Americans is even higher: sixty-nine percent during the years 1970–1990.

Massive reports have been issued by experts who have examined the UN Secretariat in detail: All put forward a great many recommendations on how to improve standards. But reform of administrative procedures and management techniques is not enough, unless the Secretary-General is in fact permitted the authority on staff recruitment and management policy he was meant to have under the Charter.

The contradiction between the two concepts of the character of the Secretariat is not likely to be resolved in the foreseeable future. The Secretariat will continue to be a mixture as it is today: an extension of the intergovernmental system with elements of an independent international body. A strengthening of the independent elements and raising the morale and quality of the service will be difficult to achieve unless and until the governments of the major powers take the UN more seriously. This may now be happening. The use of UN services in the Persian Gulf proves that the Organization is needed for important operational tasks.

The "limits" will always be there, but the scope for independent action by the Secretary-General varies in accordance with changes in the constellation of world power. During the Cold War, the limits were set by the relations between the United States and the Soviet Union. At times of tension the Secretary-General had to lie low so as not to be caught in the crossfire between the two superpowers; in times of détente he had to carry out their joint decisions. From now on, the Secretary-General should have more opportunity to widen the limits. Moscow has finally overcome its Hammarskjöld-phobia and no longer dogmatically opposes a more independent role for the Secretary-General. The bipolar order is giving way to a more dispersed pattern of power. The non-aligned group, too, has ceased to be a compact lobby determined to run the Organization. The Secretary-General will have more room to maneuver.

New Qualifications

He will, however, also have to cope with a more demanding agenda. In addition to the traditional concerns of international security such as peacekeeping, good offices and preventive diplomacy, newer issues are likely to command an ever greater part of his attention: environmental crises, industrial and natural disasters, drugs, migrations. He will not be able to leave to others to deal with the central problems of economic development and the environment. And he will have to lead the restructuring of the Organization to improve its ability to meet the demands of a changing world.

In short, the new global situation requires a different type of personality as Secretary-General. The unwritten rules by which the Secretary-General has been selected until now must be reconsidered.

The first rule has been to look, not only for the right person, but for the right person from the right country. Only nationals of neutral or non-aligned states have been considered eligible. In a bipolar order, this made sense. It minimized the risk of a Secretary-General being caught in a conflict of interest between his international duties and his natural loyalty toward his native country.

This neutrality clause was challenged by Soviet leader Khrushchev in his dramatic feud with Hammarskjöld. "There are neutral countries, but no neutral men," he told Walter Lippman in 1961. In his celebrated rebuttal, Hammarskjöld admitted that the issue of the impartiality of an international civil servant raised "a serious intellectual and moral problem." He said:

> "We have to deal here with a question of integrity or with, if you please, a question of conscience. . . . The international civil servant is not requested to be a neuter in the sense that he has to have no sympathies or antipathies, that there are to be no interests which are close to him in his personal capacity or that he is to have no ideas or ideals that matter for him. However, he is requested to be fully aware of those human reactions and meticulously check himself that they are not permitted to influence his actions."[8]

What Hammarskjöld was saying was that personal integrity was more important than nationality, and my own experiences of dealing with persons of different nationalities in international organizations bear him out. During the ten years of U Thant's two terms, the political function of the UN was in fact run by an American and an Englishman

— Ralph Bunche and Brian Urquhart — neither of whom could ever be suspected of putting the interests of his native country above those of the UN.

Nationality cannot of course be completely discounted in the selection of the Secretary-General. Clearly, a national of a state involved in a conflict would have to be ruled out. But in future more emphasis could be placed on the person and less on his nationality, which would widen the field of possible candidates. As the East-West conflict loses its sharp edges, the distinction between neutrals and lesser allies becomes blurred, and both superpowers will be able to take a more relaxed view of the nationality qualification.

Yet there is another view which supports the notion that the election of the Secretary-General should be made subject to rotation among the regional groups. Since so far Europe has had the post three times, Asia once and Latin America once, it is agreed that an African should be next in line. The adoption of such a procedure would, in my view, be a fatal blow to the independence of the Secretary-General, who would be perceived as representing his constituency rather than the membership as a whole. An African could certainly be elected, but he must be elected on his personal qualifications, not as a nominee of the African group.

The second unwritten rule hitherto observed in the election of the Secretary-General can be deduced from the professional background of those appointed. With the exception of Trygve Lie, all four Secretaries-General had had a career in diplomacy. U Thant, Waldheim, and Pérez de Cuellar had actually served as representatives of their countries in the UN itself, while Hammarskjöld, too, had earned his reputation in the field of multilateral diplomacy.

That the post of Secretary-General is a job for a diplomat, preferably one with UN experience, has been taken for granted. Diplomacy, being the art of the possible, teaches one to work within the limits set by the realities of power. The Secretary-General spends most of his time working with the representatives of the member states — other diplomats. His daily task is to harmonize diverse or conflicting interests, smooth over differences and mediate in disputes ranging from the trivial to the deadly. For this he needs the negotiating experience and the verbal skills, the discretion and infinite patience of a first-rate diplomat.

But are the qualities and skills acquired in a diplomatic career still sufficient by themselves? I believe the next Secretary-General will need a number of qualifications not normally associated with diplomats. He must be able and willing to take political initiatives without waiting for instructions. Ideally he should have an understanding of the economic forces that now shape international relations. Above all he will have to be able to appeal over the heads of governments to public opinion in the major countries, especially in the United States. The Secretary-General commands an unusually visible pulpit — a word used by the UNA report — from which to attract attention, especially interest of the media. So far it has not been used effectively. U Thant was prone to preach sermons on the theme of tolerance; Waldheim was keen on self-promotion; Pérez de Cuellar has been self-effacing to the point of invisibility. In this age of media power the diplomatic virtue of discretion has turned into a liability. What John Maynard Keynes said in 1919 about the League of Nations is still valid about the UN: "The League will operate by its influence on the public opinion of the world."[9]

There are physical as well as political limits to what a Secretary-General can do. He must carry a heavy burden of representational and ceremonial duties. Custom requires his presence at numerous meetings of UN bodies, and he has to spend considerable time away from New York attending conferences in different parts of the world. The ability to delegate must be very high on the list of the qualifications for the next Secretary-General.

The UN needs a leader with the courage and vision to venture into the unknown territory that lies beyond the safety of precedent and custom. What could induce the governments of the five permanent members of the Security Council to choose such a person? The tradition has been to leave the Five, like a college of secular cardinals, to haggle behind closed doors, while the rest of the UN anxiously waits for the smoke signal announcing the election of a new pope. In a study sponsored by the Ford Foundation and the Dag Hammarskjöld Foundation, Brian Urquhart and Erskine Childers propose an "improved process of appointment," including the establishment of a search group with the task of finding candidates, in order to avoid a repetition of the haphazard procedure that in 1971 led to the appointment of Waldheim. Pérez de Cuellar has gone so far as to insist that "no person should ever be a candidate, declared or undeclared, for this office. It is a post that should come unsought to a qualified person."[10] Only in this way, he believes, the impartiality of the Secretary-General could remain untainted by any feeling of indebtedness to governments which may have supported his appointment.

Unfortunately we are not likely to return to an age of chivalry. It will not be possible to depoliticize the process of selecting a Secretary-General. There will always be opportunism, rumor, gossip and intrigue. There will always be candidates, declared and undeclared. Indeed, in my view, all the candidates should declare themselves publicly. As Brian Urquhart has pointed out, "Looking for the person with the qualities best suited for this infinitely demanding and important job seems to hold a very low priority for governments. Rather, political differences dictate a search for a candidate who will not exert any troubling degree of leadership, commitment, originality or independence."[11] The five governments, if left to make the decision in secret conclave, are likely to reach down to the lowest common denominator, and the odds are against their repeating the mistake of picking another Hammarskjöld. The only force that could persuade them to accept an outstanding person is the pressure of informed public opinion, a force that can only make itself felt if all candidates are exposed in advance to public scrutiny. I am not so naive as to believe that such a procedure would necessarily ensure the election of the strongest candidate, but it would at least reduce the risk that a mediocrity is chosen.

Limits will always be there. As ambassador Max Finger, a former member of the US mission to the UN, has put it, what is required in the Secretary-General is "excellence within the parameters of political reality." It is time to put the emphasis on excellence rather than on the parameters. The choice of the next Secretary-General will in fact be a crucial test for the governments of the major powers: Do they really mean what they say when they proclaim their desire to revitalize the UN?

Conclusions

The test for the UN, as for all institutions, lies in the hackneyed question: If it did not exist, would we have to invent it? My answer is, yes, the world needs the UN because there are essential tasks only a global organization can perform. But if we had to invent such an organization today, it would not be an exact copy of the one that grew out of the barrel of the gun in 1945. We would not delegate to a gang of five supranational powers to use armed force for the purpose of maintaining law and order in the world. Our understanding of the nature of international security has broadened, since 1945, to take into account other factors besides the military ones. Instead of putting the emphasis on enforcement powers, we would create a service-oriented organization designed to assist governments in a common effort to maintain peace. We would avoid, I hope, making the mistake of creating a mock parliament that lacks both authority and responsibility. We would wish to construct an assembly that would act as a negotiating body seeking consensus and mutual understanding.

The UN is in fact evolving in these directions. The question is what could be done to give this process of adaptation a coherent conceptual frame.

The essential tasks only the UN as a global organization can perform on behalf of all its member states can be grouped under three general headings: First, the UN is a permanent diplomatic market for the exchange of information and views. It is a meeting-place for the representatives of the governments of all the world's states; a forum for debate, a safety-valve, a wailing wall, a platform from which victims of aggression and injustice can appeal to world public opinion. Second, the UN is the instrument by which governments seek to reach a consensus on guidelines for common action on global issues. Through the UN nations are able to define and codify norms and standards of civilized relations between states, develop public international law and promote observance of universal principles of human rights within states. Third, the UN provides member states with a number of important services, for the purpose of maintaining international peace and security as well as for a number of other common purposes, such as humanitarian assistance for refugees and victims of natural or manmade disasters.

This three-point concept of the functions of the UN is not likely to satisfy those who believe that the UN should be the center from which "a strategy of global change" is directed and managed. I believe that such a role is unattainable in the foreseeable future, and I am not convinced that it is desirable. There are indeed global problems, but the action that has to be taken to solve them is for the most part regional, national or local. Interdependence has not put an end to the diversity of mankind. Governments cooperate with each other within several concentric circles of neighbors, allies, trading partners and ideological kin, and the UN is bound to be on the outer circle.

In view of the changes that have transformed the international system during the past fifty years it is only natural that the UN is in part antiquated and in need of modernization. The conventional wisdom is that reforms must be carried out without Charter revision. It must be born in mind that the Charter was adopted at a moment in history when solidarity within the victorious alliance was at its height. Only two or three years later it would have been difficult to reach general agreement on such a text. The argument is that any attempt to rewrite it today in a manner that would satisfy the five permanent members of the Security Council as well as two-thirds of all member states, as required for revisions, might end in deadlock. Were we to take the Charter apart we might find it difficult to put it together again. Charter revision, according to this view, would inevitably open a Pandora's box of diverse and conflicting demands that might undermine the very foundations of the Organization. And finally, the Soviet government has been opposed to revision, presumably because it has feared it might lead to an attack on the veto.

The UN has in fact been able to adapt its procedures and organization to meet changing demands without formally rewriting the Charter. Peacekeeping, an activity not mentioned in the Charter, is an outstanding example, the new mechanism for making budget decisions is another. A great deal more can be done without touching the Charter.

To begin with, the governments of member states could start paying their dues in full and on time. At present the Organization is leading a hand-to-mouth existence. "The possibility of imminent bankruptcy has been my constant preoccupation," Secretary-General stated in December 1990. At that time only sixty-four member states had fully paid their assessed contributions to the regular budget, while ninety-three member states were in arrears and twenty-four had made no payments at all.

The situation will gradually improve, as the United States continues to pay its arrears of half a billion dollars over the next few years. By withholding funds the United States achieved its purpose of forcing the General Assembly to adopt budget procedures that ensure fiscal responsibility. Budget proposals are now voted by a committee of 18 nations including all the main contributors, and since decisions are made by consensus, the United States and the other major powers now in effect have a veto over expenditures. As a result, the budget for the two years 1990-1991, amounting to close to two billion dollars, is lower in real terms than total expenditures for the previous two years and staff reductions undertaken since 1986 are now nearing the recommended target of fifteen percent.

Administrative reform is a continuing process, and no doubt more cuts will be made. But the time has come to turn from across the board reductions to qualitative reform. Again, this can be carried out without changing the Charter. Indeed, a qualitative improvement in the administration of the UN can only be achieved if and when the governments of member states begin to show greater respect for Article 100 of the Charter which lays down the principles of an independent international civil service. The Secretary-General must be allowed to run the Secretariat and make appointments with greater independence. Financial security and greater administrative efficiency will be needed to improve the capacity of the UN to respond to the growing demand for peace- keeping services as well as various kinds of assistance to countries in distress.

There is, however, a limit to what can be achieved without Charter revision. Now that the Soviet leadership is engaged in an effort to restructure its own society it may no longer object to a modest perestroika in the UN. The view that any attempt at Charter revision might endanger the entire structure seems to me overly defeatist. A restructuring of the principal organs of the UN is urgently needed and this cannot be accomplished without changing the Charter.

The Trusteeship Council, which has had responsibility for supervising the administration of former colonies until they gain independence, has run out of customers. Only one tiny island territory in the Pacific Ocean remains under its care. A decision to abolish the Council would mark the formal end of the colonial era as the world has known it.

A Soviet proposal to turn the Trusteeship Council into a environmental body for the management of the global commons (the oceans, the atmosphere, biological diversity, and planetary climate) has excited a great deal of interest, but is likely to raise insuperable political problems. More practicable is the idea of reconstructing the Economic and Social Council in order to make it a more effective instrument for dealing with the whole complex of interrelated issues such as economic development, population, and ecology. How this should and could be done remains nebulous and will require a great deal more study and discussion.

A reform of the Security Council is in my view the most urgent task. Who might take the initiative? It should not come from the governments of countries aspiring to gain a permanent seat on the Council. Ideally, it should come from the present permanent members, but it may be too much to expect them to act in such a selfless manner. More likely, the Nordic countries (Denmark, Finland, Iceland, Norway and Sweden), a group committed to strengthening the UN as an agency for maintaining peace and security, could present a balanced and reasoned proposal to the UN membership.

Critics of the UN often demand that the General Assembly, too, should be reformed. Their main complaint is that the principle of one-state one-vote distorts reality. I agree that the General Assembly as it is constituted represents a misguided attempt to transplant an organ belonging to parliamentary democracy into the quite different body of an intergovernmental organization of sovereign states. But I cannot agree that a change of the voting system — by the introduction of weighted votes for instance — is the answer. The General Assembly does not, after all, make decisions that are binding on member states. Now even budget decisions have been taken away from it. A resolution adopted by the Assembly is thus comparable to an opinion poll conducted among the governments of the member states. How could a vote cast by a government in such a poll be weighted? Is the vote of a large and powerful country ruled by a dictator to be assessed as more valuable than the vote of a small democratic country?

Another idea for reforming the General Assembly is to disqualify so-called mini-states from membership on the ground that they are too small to be genuinely independent. Yet there are large nations whose independence is a sham, and small nations that have been able to assert themselves in adverse circumstances. Any attempt to define quantitative criteria for national independence is doomed to fail. In the discussion on the question on mini-states during my time on the Security Council an American delegate suggested that a country ought to have at least half a million inhabitants to qualify for UN membership. When I pointed out that this would lead to the expulsion of Iceland, an ancient nation with an impeccable record of independence, the discussion came to an end.

The ideal solution would not be to change the voting system, but to recognize that voting on resolutions dealing with substantive international issues is meaningless and should stop. Only procedural or organizational matters can be decided by vote. While no formal decision to abolish voting on substantive resolutions is likely to be taken, in practice the trend is in the direction of adopting resolutions by consensus. Of the 383 resolutions and decisions recorded during the 1988 session of the General Assembly, two thirds (245) were adopted by consensus — a sign of growing realism.[12]

Nonetheless, the United States Congress still insists on grading the behavior of other states by counting the number of times their votes in the UN coincide with those of the United States. As former US Ambassador Vernon Walters has pointed out, the statistical system used to measure voting patterns, as required by US law, fails to produce a comprehensive or accurate picture of the results of General Assembly sessions. Not only does it ignore the large number of resolutions adopted by consensus, it also is predicated on the patently absurd notion that all items on which a vote is taken are equally important. One only has to glance at the list of resolutions adopted by any one session of the General Assembly to understand that many of them have little or no impact on world public opinion.

This is of course part of the problem. Year after year, the same items reappear on the General Assembly agenda like ducks in a shooting gallery. Assembly debates are series of statements addressed to an invisible audience in the speaker's distant home country. Its resolutions are composed in a jargon that is almost incomprehensible to most people. The first representative of the Peking government to speak in the General Assembly in November 1971 warned delegates not to degrade language. The longer the resolutions, he said, the less they mean. He could have quoted Confucius who said:

> "If the prince were waiting for you to come and administer his country for him what would be your first measure? The master said, 'It would certainly be to correct the language . . . If language is incorrect, then what is said does not accord with what was meant; and if what is said does not accord with what was meant, what is to be done cannot be effected.' "

The trouble is that in the General Assembly the lack of power encourages an irresponsible use of language. The sensible thing to do would be to concentrate the agenda on a manageable number of important questions and adopt resolutions only on issues on which a consensus can be reached. But this cannot be accomplished by Charter revision: it depends on the will of the governments of the member states to use the General Assembly more effectively for common purposes.

The purposes of the UN are set out in Chapter I of the Charter. As Secretary-General Pérez de Cuellar said, "The Charter needs to be viewed not as an external and onerous appendix but as a body of principles which must govern the life of every nation," Here is the preacher telling his flock that they must observe the commandments every day, not just on Sundays. It is of course the duty of the Secretary-General to keep before the eyes of the world a vision of the Charter as a book of law governing the day-to-day behavior of all nations. This idealistic view must be tempered by awareness of the true nature of the Charter as a compact between the governments of the existing states for the preservation of the status quo with all its anachronisms, anomalies, and injustices. But it is the best that can be done in present circumstances. Some of the language now sounds a little out of date, but the same can be said of the Ten Commandments. It is doubtful that another committee of government representatives could improve on it. A poet might do better. I am reminded of a fragment of a poem by W.H. Auden:

> *You shall love your crooked neighbor with your crooked heart.*

The two lines crisply sum up the more elaborate rules of conduct prescribed by the Charter.

NOTES

Introduction

1. W. F. Moneypenny and G. E. Buckle, *The Life of Benjamin Disraeli* (London, 1929), vol. II, p. 473.

2. Karl Marx, *The Communist Manifesto* (New York: Washington Square Press, 1964), pp. 62-66.

3. "The Foreign Policy and Diplomatic Activity of the USSR, April 1985-October 1989," a survey prepared by the USSR Foreign Ministry, International Affairs, Moscow, January 1990.

4. Alastair Buchan Memorial Lecture, International Institute of Strategic Studies, London, March 20, 1986.

5. Quoted in *Der Spiegel*, November 7, 1988.

6. Werner von Simson, *Die Verteidigung des Friedens* (Verlag C.H.Beck, München, 1975), p. 15.

7. Maurice Bertrand, "The Role of the UN in Economic and Social Fields," UN Management & Decision-making project of the UN Association of the USA, 1987.

8. The phrase was often used by Lord Caradon, Britain's Permanent Representative to the UN in 1965-68.

9. Henry Kissinger, *White House Years* (Boston, Mass.: Little, Brown and Co., 1979); Kissinger, *Years of Upheaval* (Boston, Mass.: Little, Brown and Co., 1982); Zbigniev Brzezinski, *Power and Principle* (New York: Farrar, Straus & Giroux, Inc., 1983).

Chapter I

1. Ruth Russel, *A History of the United Nations Charter* (Washington, D.C.: The Brookings Institution, 1958), p. 97.

179

2. Seymour Maxwell Finger, *Your Man at the UN* (New York: New York University Press, 1980), pp. 96-101.

3. Andrew Boyd, *Fifteen Men on a Powder Keg* (London: Methuen & Co. Ltd., 1971), pp. 323-29.

4. See Conor Cruise O'Brien's brilliant essay "The United Nations--Sacred Drama" (New York: Simon and Schuster, 1968).

5. Finger, *Your Man at the UN*, p. 49.

6. Finger, *Your Man at the UN*, p. 93.

7. Brian Urquhart, *Hammarskjold* (New York: Alfred A. Knopf, 1972), p. 253.

8. Urquhart, *Hammarskjold*, p. 406.

9. Ronald Steel, *Walter Lippmann and The American Century* (Boston: Little, Brown & Co., 1980), pp. 510-12.

10. Finger, *Your Man at the UN*, p. 116.

11. Urquhart, *Hammarskjold*, p. 458.

12. Urquhart, *Hammarskjold*, p. 461.

13. U Thant, *A View from the UN* (New York: Doubleday & Co., 1978), p. 31.

14. Urquhart, *Hammarskjold*, p. 461.

15. U Thant, *A View from the UN*, p. 32.

16. U Thant, *A View from the UN*, p. 36.

17. Finger, *Your Man at the UN*, p. 171.

18. Finger, *Your Man at the UN*, pp. 161-63.

19. U Thant's memoirs contain a detailed account of his mediation effort in the Vietnam war (*A View from the UN*, pp. 57-84), without mentioning his threat to refuse re-election.

20. The history of the Non-Proliferation Treaty has been told in numerous publications. I have relied on the series of Stockholm International Peace Research Institute books on the subject, partly on my own notes, and reports from the UN.

21. Kissinger, *White House Years,* pp. 183-86.

22. Kissinger, *Years of Upheaval,* p. 447.

23. Burton Yale Pines, ed., *A World Without a UN* (Washington, D.C.: The Heritage Foundation, 1984).

24. *International Herald Tribune,* July 7, 1988.

25. Harold Nicolson, *The Congress of Vienna* (New York: The Viking Press, 1946), pp. 250-51.

26. Barbara W. Tuchman, *The Proud Tower* (New York: Macmillan Co., 1962), pp. 229-40.

27. Milovan Djilas, *Conversations with Stalin* (New York: Harcourt Brace Jovanovich, Inc., 1962), p. 114.

28. Quoted in *Moscow News,* April 5, 1989.

29. R. P. H. King, "The United Nations and The Iran-Iraq War," a Ford Foundation Conference Report with an introduction by Brian Urquhart and Gary Sick, provides an excellent summary of UN proceedings on this issue up to the summer of 1987.

30. A phrase used by Julian Perry Robinson, a leading expert on chemical warfare, quoted in *Newsweek,* January 16, 1989.

31. Report on the world arms trade in 1988 prepared by Richard F. Grimmet for the Congressional Research Service.

Chapter II

1. "Strategic Survey 1988-89," published by Brassey's for The International Institute for Strategic Studies, pp. 14-24.

2. *Survival,* May/June 1989, published by Brassey's for the International Institute for Strategic Studies, pp. 209-24.

3. *International Herald Tribune,* September 26, 1989 and October 12, 1989.

4. Stockholm International Peace Research Institute Year Book 1989, pp. 339-42.

Chapter III

1. Finger, *Your Man at the UN,* p. 96.

2. Conor Cruise O'Brien, *The Siege* (New York: Simon & Schuster, 1986), pp. 489-90.

3. *International Herald Tribune,* May 27-28, 1989.

Chapter IV

1. Bertrand, "The Role fo the UN in Economic and Social Fields."

2. Tom J. Farer, "The UN and Human Rights: More Than a Whimper, Less Than a Roar," essay in *United Nations, Divided World,* Adam Roberts and Benedict Kingsbury, eds., (New York: Oxford University Press, 1988).

3. *Die Zeit,* April 28, 1989.

4. *International Herald Tribune,* January 2, 1991.

5. Kenneth Dadzie, "The UN and the Problem of Economic Development," essay in *United Nations, Divided World,* Roberts and Kingsbury, eds.

6. Quoted by Flora Lewis in the *International Herald Tribune,* October 31, 1988.

7. *International Herald Tribune,* September 2, 1988.

8. Dadzie, "The UN and the Problem of Economic Development," from *United Nations, Divided World,* Roberts and Kingsbury, eds.

9. Quoted by Tom Wicker in the *International Herald Tribune,* September 6, 1989.

10. World Commission on Employment & Development Staff, *Our Common Future* (New York: Oxford University Press, 1987), p. 8.

11. "The State of International Organization, 1988", report by Donald Puckala and Roger Coate, issued by the Academic Council on the UN System, June 1988.

12. Report of the World Institute for Development Economics Research Study Group, World Economic Summits, series no. 4, May 1989.

13. An account of all these proposals can be found in the UNA report cited above.

Chapter V

1. Russel, *A History of the United Nations Charter,* p. 860.

2. Urquhart, *Hammarskjold,* p. 251.

3. Brian Urquhart, *Life in Peace and War* (New York: Harper & Row, 1987), p. 228.

4. U Thant, *A View from the UN,* p. 32.

5. Javier Pérez de Cuellar, "The Role of the Secretary-General," essay in *United Nations, Divided World,* Roberts and Kingsbury, eds.

6. U Thant, *A View from the UN,* p. 33.

7. Barbara Tuchman, *The March of Folly* (London: Michael Joseph, 1984).

8. Urquhart, *Hammarskjold,* pp. 528-29.

9. Quoted by Shirley Hazzard in the *New Yorker,* September 25, 1989.

10. Pérez de Cuellar, "The Role of the Secretary-General," essay in *United Nations, Divided World,* Roberts and Kingsbury, eds.

11. Urquhart, *Life in Peace and War,* pp. 227-28.

12. State Department report to Congress on Voting Practices in the UN (Washington, D.C.: Government Printing Office, April 20, 1989), I-3-5.

INDEX